CW00869445

People and the Environment

Peter Bond

Blackwell Education

First published 1989

© Peter Bond 1989

Published by Basil Blackwell Ltd
108 Cowley Road
Oxford OX4 1JF
England

All rights reserved. No part of this system may be reproduced, stored in a retrieval system, or transmitted, in any form or by any means, electronic, mechanical, photocopying, recording or otherwise, without the prior permission of Basil Blackwell Ltd.

British Library Cataloguing in Publication Data
Bond, Peter
  People and the Environment
  1. Human Geography
  I. Title
  304.2
ISBN 0 631 90151 5

Acknowledgements

Australia High Commission 11E; Barnaby's Picture Library 10B, 26B, 52B; Birmingham City Council 58C; H Bolton Seed 9A; Peter Bond 1A, 1B, 14F, 43C; Bournemouth Evening Echo 15C; Cambridge University Committee for Aerial Photography 38D; Camera Press 41B, 59A, 59D, 61J; Central Electricity Generating Board 53C; Countryside Commission 36A, 37D; Daily Telegraph Colour Library 60D; G James/Merthyr Tydfil Public Library 56C; Japan Tourist Office 4B; Eric Kay 40B; Frank Lane 6C, 20A, 20D, 22C; London Scientific Services 49B; National Metereological Library 23D; National Remote Sensing Centre 19B, 48C, 48D; Cliff Ollier 5C; Oxfam 8E, 24B, 25C, 35D, 42B, 51A; Panos Pictures 32B; David Parker/ Science Photo Library 21B, 54C; Popperfoto 16A, 56B; Seychelles Tourist Office 39C; Graham Topping 11C; Travel Photo International 7C; United States Department of Agriculture 30B, 31C; United States Soil Conservation Service 26D, 30D; Allan Wilcox 44B; Wood Visual Communications 18A.

The author and publishers would also like to thank the following for permission to extract written material or to re-draw illustrations:
Daily Telgraph 21D, 42D, 43E; Guardian Newspapers 22H, 37B, 57B; Soviet Weekly 7B, 57B; Times Newspapers 2D, 23E, 51B, 52D, 54A.

Designed by Bob Prescott Design Assoc., Oxford
Phototypesetting by Opus, Oxford
Printed in Hong Kong by Wing King Tong Co. Ltd.

Contents

Introduction

THIS BOOK IS intended to meet the needs of teachers following GCSE syllabuses which include sections or modules concerned with the complex relationship between people and their environment. The people-environment theme has become popular in recent years, though the emphasis and approaches vary with different syllabuses. *People and the Environment* has been written with this variety in mind.

The book follows the GCSE National Criteria by presenting a wide range of local, national and international studies, although more space has been devoted to the United Kingdom than any other country. These studies are designed to develop an awareness in pupils of the ways in which people interact with the natural environment in different parts of the world, and the ways in which people can influence the natural processes which affect the development of environments. In so doing, it is hoped that pupils will develop a sensitive awareness of environmental issues and discover the difficulties faced by decision-makers and managers in our modern world.

There are three sections in the book. The first section covers the influence of the natural environment on human activity. General background information on geomorphology, climate, soils etc. is provided where necessary to aid pupils' understanding of natural processes.

The second section covers the increasingly significant role of people as agents of change in the environment.

Section three includes further, more detailed case studies of the interaction between people and the natural environment. This section is intended for use with more able (or more interested) pupils since it extends the work covered in the first two sections.

Each section is written so that it should be comprehensible to the vast majority of GCSE pupils. A wide range of data and questions is presented in order to encourage active learning rather than simple absorption of a body of knowledge.

Each section is intended to test not only acquisition of factual knowledge, but also understanding, analysis and interpretation of data. Questions are based upon those used by GCSE examination boards. They are graded in order of difficulty. Some of the more complex later questions are not intended for use with less able pupils – teachers must decide how to use these questions according to the nature of the teaching group.

Key geographical terms are set in bold type in the text to make identification easier. Many of these terms are explained in sufficient detail in the relevant unit, but a glossary of the most widely used geographical terms has been provided for pupil reference at the back of the book.

1 : People and the Environment

LOOK AROUND YOU. Everything you see makes up your immediate **environment**. Outside this area is a much larger and more variable environment of trees, grass, roads, houses and so on. Some features such as mountains are obviously natural, and others such as roads are obviously man-made. But are we always right when we make this distinction?

Planet Earth is thought to be about 4.6 billion (4,600,000,000) years old. Through most of its history, there have been no people on the Earth. The Human Race (Homo Sapiens) has been on Earth for less than 50,000 years.

Until a few thousand years ago, people were hunters and gatherers and their total number was less than 100 million (100,000,000). This population lived in balance with the natural environment, increasing in times of plenty and decreasing in times of famine, disease and other natural disasters. Changes to the environment generally took place slowly and were small in scale.

This balance began to change as people developed ways of changing the natural environment, clearing forests, damming and diverting rivers, mining for natural resources and creating permanent settlements. The rate of change has been especially rapid in the last 200 years and there are now 5 billion people on Earth.

Modern technology and machines have meant a rapid expansion of human influence on the environment. Today, there are few parts of the world where there is a truly natural environment, untouched by humans. Trees and grass have often been planted or sown by people. Marsh or desert may be turned into fertile farmland. A large river may be deepened or straightened for ships and barges – but it can equally well be turned into a smelly, lifeless sewer full of chemicals and waste.

1 **a** Look around you. Describe your immediate environment.

b Now think about your local environment – the area where you live. Which features would you describe as natural, and which features as man-made? Give examples of each type.

c Make a list of any local features which appear to be natural but have been introduced or modified by people at some time.

d Look at an old map of your area. Compare it with a modern map. Make a list of the changes that have taken place.

e Look at your list from (d). Suggest why those changes took place. Do you think they have been good or bad? Give reasons for your answer.

2 **a** What are the main uses of the environment in **A** and **B**?

b How are people trying to improve the environment in **B**?

c For each photograph, make a list of the main features visible (trees, smoke, houses etc.) Give each feature a score based on your ideas about its appearance and attractiveness. Use these numbers:

−2 Bad, −1 Poor, 0 Neutral, +1 Good, +2 Excellent.

Add up the totals for each picture.

d Which picture gained the highest score? How did other members of the class score the pictures? What does this tell you about man-modified environments?

A A man-made rural environment

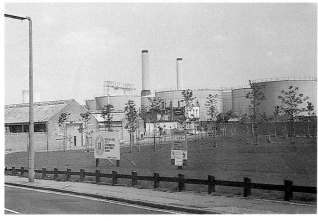

B A man-made urban environment

2 : The Nature of Disasters

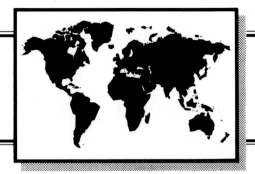

EVERY YEAR, thousands of people are killed or injured by catastrophic natural events or man-made disasters, while the cost of damage to crops, buildings and other property runs into billions of pounds. Such disasters can take place anywhere in the world, but they are rarely reported from remote or sparsely-populated areas where they have little impact on human activity. On the other hand, the areas most at risk are the densely-populated tropics. There, people are crowded into sites which are vulnerable to such hazards as tropical storms, floods, earthquakes and drought.

What makes a disaster? Events which result in loss of life and/or great destruction of property are classified as disasters. They usually result from a sudden, unpredictable event such as a landslide or earthquake. People who are affected may not be aware of the danger until after the event, although this is not always the case. Those living in the active earthquake zone of California *are* aware of the probability of a major quake at some time in the future, but they are willing to accept the risk and continue to live in those areas. In such cases, the authorities can only take all possible safety measures and set up early warning systems. **C** shows the reasons why people decide to take action.

The Nature of Disasters

Disasters can be classified according to:
- their magnitude or scale as measured by number of deaths and cost of damage.
- their frequency of occurrence.
- the suddenness with which they arrive.
- the length of time during which they occur.

As **A** shows, most natural disasters tend to be much less frequent than man-made disasters such as plane crashes or motorway crashes. However, natural disasters also tend to be more destructive and cause a higher loss of life. This is because they cover a much larger area and involve huge amounts of energy. For example, the energy released when Mount St Helens volcano erupted has been compared with the detonation of 27,000 Hiroshima-size atom bombs.

Not all disasters can be clearly classified as natural or man-made. There have been many cases where natural forces have combined with the effects of human activity to create a disaster (**B**). People settling near known earthquake and volcano hazard zones is one example. The creation of smog is another. These disasters could be prevented by changes in human practices, but natural disasters tend to be beyond human control.

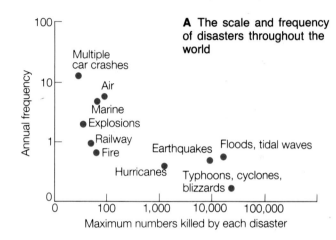

A The scale and frequency of disasters throughout the world

Reducing the Likelihood of Disaster

The only sure way to reduce loss of life and property damage from natural disasters is to stop people living in or using potential hazard zones. Often, though, whole countries can be vulnerable, so there is nowhere safe to which people could move.

The other main problems are poverty and lack of choice. Most people in the poor, developing countries rely on the land for their food and survival. If they leave the land, perhaps to go to the city, they may end up begging on the streets with no house, no food, no money, no job and no family to support them. So the rice farmers of the Ganges delta stay on the fertile land, despite the knowledge that a cyclone may strike in the near future, wiping out all of their hard work and threatening their lives.

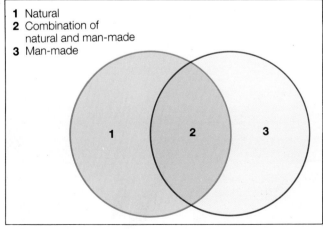

1 Natural
2 Combination of natural and man-made
3 Man-made

B Classification of disasters

1 Study **A**, then answer these questions:
a Which three disasters occur most frequently?
b Which disasters occur least frequently?
c Which is the most frequent natural disaster?
d Which disasters cause the greatest loss of life?

2 Using the classification in **B**, list these disasters under the most appropriate heading:
a Motorway pile-up caused by lorry jack-knifing.
b Motorway pile-up caused by thick fog.
c Ocean liner sinks after striking iceberg.
d Hotel for skiers destroyed in avalanche.
e People drowned in river flood.
f Earthquake destroys roads and bridges in rural area.
g City is destroyed by the first hurricane to hit the area in 100 years.
h People die from breathing problems in smog.
i People die from drinking factory waste in water.
j Early blizzard strikes farmers and kills crops and livestock.

3 Study **D**. Note that the British Meteorological Office did not forecast the severity of the storm.
a Was this a natural or man-made disaster, or a mixture of both? Give reasons for your answer.
b What was the average wind speed on the Beaufort Scale?
c Suggest why the severity of the storm was not accurately forecast.

d How many people died? Which, if any, of these deaths might have been avoided if the storm had been accurately forecast?
e Many more would have died if it had struck in daylight. Why?

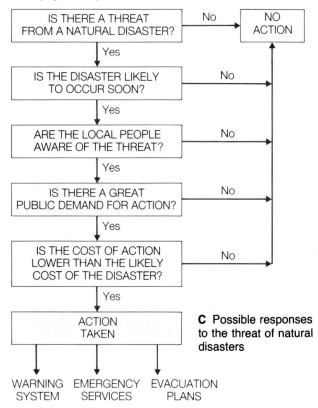

C Possible responses to the threat of natural disasters

WARNING SYSTEM   EMERGENCY SERVICES   EVACUATION PLANS

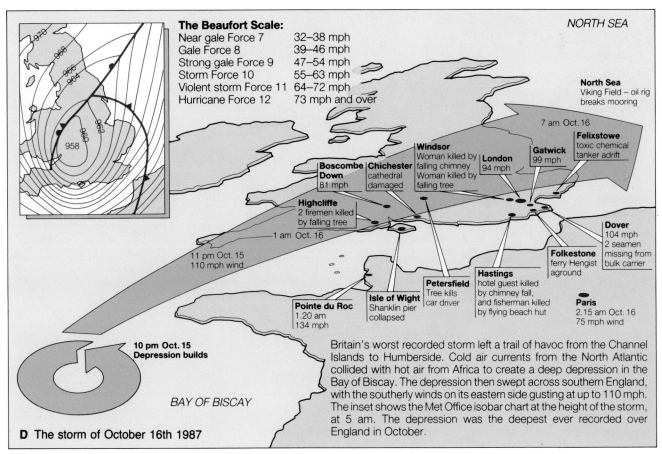

The Beaufort Scale:

Near gale Force 7	32–38 mph
Gale Force 8	39–46 mph
Strong gale Force 9	47–54 mph
Storm Force 10	55–63 mph
Violent storm Force 11	64–72 mph
Hurricane Force 12	73 mph and over

NORTH SEA

North Sea
Viking Field – oil rig breaks mooring

7 am Oct.16

Felixstowe
toxic chemical tanker adrift

Windsor
Woman killed by falling chimney
Woman killed by falling tree

London
94 mph

Gatwick
99 mph

Boscombe Down
81 mph

Chichester
cathedral damaged

Highcliffe
2 firemen killed by falling tree

Dover
104 mph
2 seamen missing from bulk carrier

1 am Oct.16

Folkestone
ferry Hengist aground

11 pm Oct.15
110 mph wind

Hastings
hotel guest killed by chimney fall, and fisherman killed by flying beach hut

Petersfield
Tree kills car driver

Isle of Wight
Shanklin pier collapsed

Pointe du Roc
1.20 am
134 mph

Paris
2.15 am Oct.16
75 mph wind

10 pm Oct.15
Depression builds

BAY OF BISCAY

D The storm of October 16th 1987

Britain's worst recorded storm left a trail of havoc from the Channel Islands to Humberside. Cold air currents from the North Atlantic collided with hot air from Africa to create a deep depression in the Bay of Biscay. The depression then swept across southern England, with the southerly winds on its eastern side gusting at up to 110 mph. The inset shows the Met Office isobar chart at the height of the storm, at 5 am. The depression was the deepest ever recorded over England in October.

3 : Inside the Earth

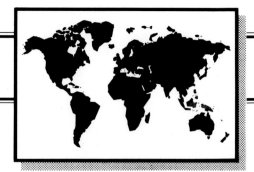

IF WE ARE going to understand the causes of natural disasters such as earthquakes and volcanic eruptions, we need to look inside planet Earth. This is not easy: the deepest hole ever drilled into the Earth is only about 11 km deep. However, shock waves from large earthquakes can pass through the planet and be detected by sensitive instruments called **seismographs**. Studies of the different types of earthquake waves have shown that there are layers within the Earth, rather like X-rays show the hidden outlines of our bones.

B shows the four major layers within the Earth. Earth has had an outer crust for more than 4 billion (4,000,000,000) years, but this solid surface is continually changing. About 70% of the surface is the ocean floor: the large land masses called **continents** make up the remainder of the surface.

Continental Drift A glance at the shapes of the continents of Africa, Europe, North America and South America suggests that they would fit together quite well. This led to the idea that the continents once did fit together, but then had moved apart – the theory of **continental drift**. However, it was very difficult to prove. The theory has only been accepted in recent years, because new methods of exploring the ocean floor and measuring the ages of rocks have provided detailed information.

Continental drift is now considered to be part of the theory of **Plate Tectonics**. Geologists believe that Earth's crust is like a huge jigsaw puzzle. Each piece of the jigsaw puzzle is called a **crustal plate**. There are seven major plates and a number of smaller ones (**A**). These plates may be made of continental or ocean crust. They 'float' on the denser, plastic mantle like giant rafts jostling against each other, and they seem to be dragged along by slow convection currents in the upper mantle (**D**). Such movements are very slow – about the same rate as your finger nails grow – but they are the cause of most earthquakes and volcanic eruptions.

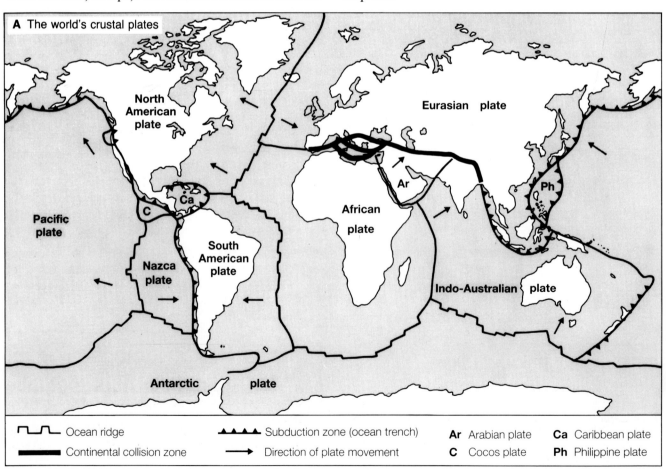

A The world's crustal plates

North American plate

Eurasian plate

Pacific plate

Ar

African plate

Ph

Ca

C

South American plate

Nazca plate

Indo-Australian plate

Antarctic plate

⊓⊔ Ocean ridge	▲▲▲ Subduction zone (ocean trench)	**Ar** Arabian plate **Ca** Caribbean plate
▬ Continental collision zone	→ Direction of plate movement	**C** Cocos plate **Ph** Philippine plate

Earthquakes and volcanoes are found where plates meet. There are three types of plate movement.

- Plates may move apart. This allows **magma** (liquid rock beneath the surface) from the mantle to force its way through cracks to the ocean floor, forming **ocean ridges** and volcanic islands.
- Plates may move towards each other. When dense ocean crust moves towards a lighter continent, the heavier ocean crust is forced down into the mantle where it melts (**C**). These **subduction zones** are marked by very deep **ocean trenches**. They produce chains of volcanoes and zones of severe earthquakes.
  Sometimes two continents move towards each other. Because they are so light, neither continent can be forced down into the mantle, so they collide, creating belts of fold mountains and earthquakes.
- Plates may slide past each other. When plates move in exactly opposite directions on either side of a **fault** (fracture) in the crust, the friction between them can cause severe earthquakes.

(a)

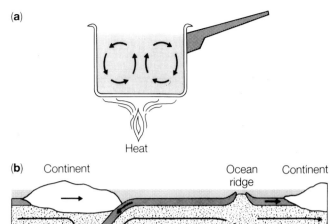

Heat

D Convection currents (a) in a pan of soup
(b) in the upper mantle

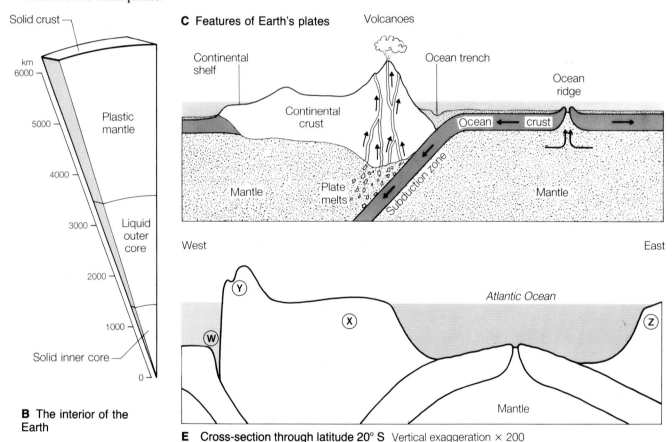

B The interior of the Earth

C Features of Earth's plates

E Cross-section through latitude 20° S Vertical exaggeration × 200

1 Write a sentence explaining the meaning of each of these terms:
a crust **b** mantle **c** magma **d** subduction zone **e** crustal plate.
2 **a** From an atlas, trace the outlines of Europe, Greenland, Africa, North America and South America. Cut around each one and move the pieces until you think they fit together fairly well.
b Explain what is meant by continental drift and how it may take place.
3 Draw a large copy of **E**, then, with the the help of an atlas:
a name ocean **W**, continent **X**, mountain range **Y** and continent **Z**.
b label an ocean ridge and an ocean trench.
c add arrows to show the direction of movement of the plates.
d use the symbol * to show where earthquakes are likely, and the symbol ▲ to show where volcanoes are likely to be found.

4 : Volcanoes

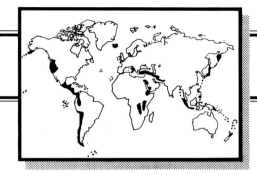

A TYPICAL VOLCANO is a mountain made from **lava** (molten surface rock) and ash. There are about 500 active volcanoes in the world, although only 20 to 30 erupt each year. Not all volcanoes are alike or erupt in the same way. Most volcanoes are of the **composite type** (**A**). They are roughly cone shaped with a large hollow (called a *crater*) at the top of the cone. A few volcanoes are made almost entirely of lava.

When a volcano erupts, **magma** (molten underground rock) pushes towards the surface. Clouds of ash and steam as well as lava come out of a hole or **vent** in the crater. These build up in layers so that the volcano grows larger with each **eruption**.

A volcanic eruption can last for as little as an hour or for more than a year. During the eruption the volcano is **active**, but it then becomes **dormant** until the next period of activity. During this quiet period, the lava in the crater solidifies, plugging the vent. Gas pressure builds up inside the volcano until a new vent opens up and another eruption begins. This may happen with a sudden explosion if the lava is **viscous** (thick and pasty) and holds a lot of gas (see **F**).

If a volcano has not been active for many centuries, it is labelled **extinct** – though supposedly extinct volcanoes have come to life again. Helgafell volcano in Iceland had been dormant for more than 5000 years when it erupted in 1973.

A The structure of a volcano (composite type)

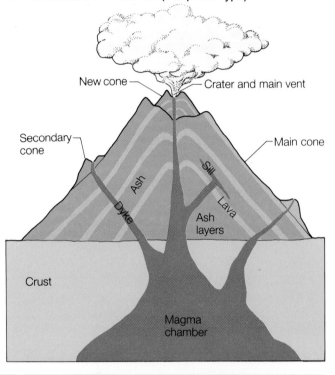

New cone

Crater and main vent

Secondary cone

Main cone

Ash

Dyke

Sill

Lava

Ash layers

Crust

Magma chamber

Shield volcano
(not explosive)

Composite volcano
(sometimes explosive)

Acid lava volcano
(very explosive)

NOT TO SCALE

E Types of volcanoes

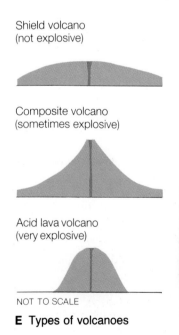

B Mount Fuji in Japan ▶

C Location of the world's active volcanoes

Volcanoes are found in narrow belts, usually close to plate boundaries. Some volcanoes are located in sparsely-populated parts of the world, so the eruption may hardly be noticed, as in the 1912 eruption of Mount Katmai in Alaska.

Unfortunately, many active volcanoes are located near areas of dense population. The islands of south-east Asia are among the most densely populated in the world, yet explosive eruptions regularly occur from the numerous volcanoes with very high death rates as a result.

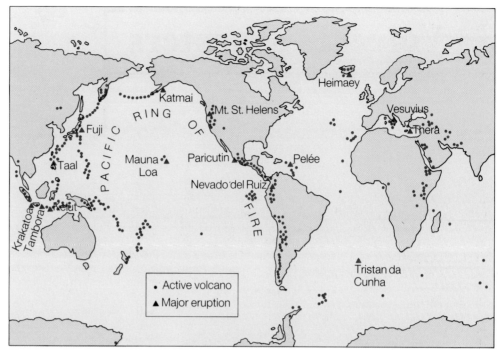

D The location of Paricutin

Birth Of A Volcano

On 5 February 1943, earthquakes shook the State of Michoacan in Mexico and continued for two weeks. On the afternoon of 20 February, an Indian farmer named Pulido was ploughing in a field when he heard underground rumblings from a small pit. Suddenly, he saw there was a fissure (crack) nearly a metre long through the pit. The field began to tremble, then sulphur-laden smoke and sparks began to come from the fissure and nearby pine trees began to burn.

By midnight, huge glowing rocks were being hurled into the air, and by 8 am the next day a volcanic cone more than 10m high had formed. Later that day came the first lava; the noise could be heard over 160 km away.

During the first few months of eruption the volcano was ejecting lava, cinders and ash at an average rate of 2700 tonnes per minute as well as another several thousand tonnes of steam every day. At the same time, everything within 8 km was covered with black ash up to 3m thick. Fine dust even fell in Mexico City, 320 km distant (**D**). The cloud of ash and steam reached an altitude of several kilometres, volcanic bombs shot high into the air and cherry-red lava flows stretched up to 10 km long.

When the eruption ended after 9 years and 12 days, the volcano, now named Paricutin, was 500m high and had ejected 3500 million tonnes of solid material, of which about a quarter was lava. Surprisingly, perhaps, no-one was killed.

1 Write a sentence explaining each of these terms:
   a crater, **b** vent, **c** lava, **d** magma, **e** extinct, **f** dormant.

2 **a** With the help of a world population density map in an atlas, list the 15 major eruptions shown on **C** under the headings ● densely populated ● moderately populated, or ● sparsely populated.
   b With the help of **A** on p8, explain the distribution of volcanoes shown in **C**.
   c Why are there no active volcanoes in Britain?

3 Look at the photograph of Mt Fuji in Japan (**B**).
   a What type of volcano do you think it is? Give reasons for your answer.
   b Would you expect Mt Fuji to be a danger to people living nearby or a major tourist attraction? Explain your answer.

4 Using the information given in the section on Paricutin, draw and label at least **three** diagrams to show the stages in the birth of a volcano.

5 Use your library to find out about the eruption of the undersea volcano which created the new island of Surtsey off the coast of Iceland in 1963. How does the birth of a new volcanic island compare with the birth of a continental volcano such as Paricutin?

F The Two Main Types of Lava.	
Basaltic Lava (Basic)	**Andesitic Lava** (Acid)
High temperature (average 1000°C).	Lower temperature (700°C).
Non-viscous (runny).	Viscous (pasty).
Thin, fast moving lava.	Thick, slow moving lava.
No explosive activity.	Explosive eruption.
Little ash produced.	Large amounts of ash.
Near ocean ridges and hot spots.	Near ocean trenches.

5 : Volcanic Disasters

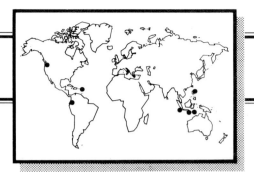

VOLCANOES ARE capable of killing many thousands of people and of causing millions of pounds worth of damage (**A**). The scale of the disaster depends on:

- the population density of the area;
- the economic value of the area;
- the type and energy release of the eruption; and
- the amount of warning given of an eruption.

A volcanic eruption can cause death and destruction through lava flows, clouds of volcanic ash, glowing gas clouds (nuées ardentes) and poisonous gases. Sometimes there are also devastating side-effects from mudflows and tidal waves (**B**). Local economies may be badly hit by famine and epidemics after food and water supplies are destroyed.

Lava Flows Although lava flows can cause a lot of damage to crops and property, they rarely cause deaths. By the time the lava reaches the lower slopes of the mountain, the local population has usually been evacuated. However, near the site of the eruption, large lumps of lava cool as they fly through the air to produce a rain of **lava bombs**.

Ash Most eruptions produce vast quantities of ash. Fine dust may be carried hundreds of kilometres from the crater by the prevailing wind. It can block out the sun and even affect the climate. Major damage can be caused close to the eruption, where the ash covers everything with a layer of 'black snow'. Settlements and fields can be buried, and buildings collapse under the weight of the ash.

B The threat from volcanoes

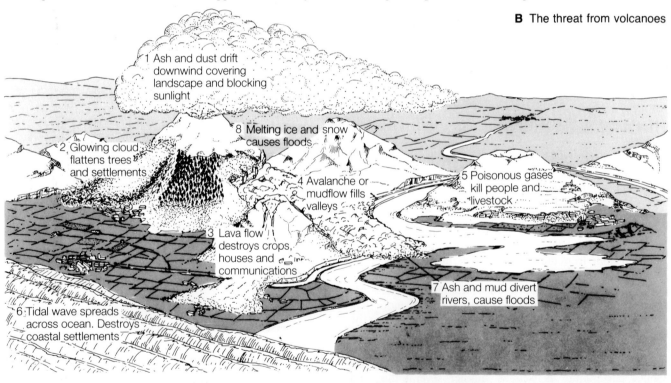

1 Ash and dust drift downwind covering landscape and blocking sunlight

8 Melting ice and snow causes floods

2 Glowing cloud flattens trees and settlements

5 Poisonous gases kill people and livestock

4 Avalanche or mudflow fills valleys

3 Lava flow destroys crops, houses and communications

7 Ash and mud divert rivers, cause floods

6 Tidal wave spreads across ocean. Destroys coastal settlements

Date	Volcano	Deaths	Causes
1470 BC	Thera, Aegean Sea	Many thousands	Explosions, tsunami
AD 79	Vesuvius, Italy	2,000?	Nuée ardente
1815	Tambora, Indonesia	82,000	Famine, epidemics
1883	Krakatoa, Indonesia	36,000	Tsunami
1902	Pelée, West Indies	30,000	Nuée ardente
1911	Taal, Philippines	1,335	Explosions
1919	Kelut, Indonesia	5,110	Mudflows
1980	Mt. St. Helens, USA	60	Nuée ardente
1985	Nevado del Ruiz, Columbia	20,000	Mudflows

A Some major volcanic disasters

12

C A glowing cloud (nuée ardente)

Glowing Clouds (Nuées Ardentes, C) When dormant volcanoes are plugged by solid lava in the vent, the gas pressure in the magma may build up. Sometimes this hot gas, filled with suspended ash, is released in a sudden explosion from the top or side of the volcano. The cloud moves down the slope at up to 200 km/hr, flattening everything in its path. Anyone breathing the fiery cloud dies almost instantly. 30,000 people died in a few minutes when a glowing cloud from Mont Pelée hit the town of St Pierre on the island of Martinique in May 1902.

Poisonous Gases Gases produced during eruptions include compounds of sulphur, carbon monoxide and carbon dioxide. These heavy gases hug the ground and can kill without warning, as happened in Cameroon in 1986 when 1500 people died during their sleep.

Mudflows Many volcanoes, even those near the Equator, are high enough above sea level to support a permanent cap of snow and ice. Eruptions rapidly melt the snow and ice, producing a sudden **flash flood**. This may be made worse by heavy rain from the thunderstorms which often occur in the clouds of ash and steam above an active volcano.

Meltwater, possibly combined with heavy rain, may mix with volcanic ash to produce a thick, pasty mudflow. This is capable of flowing rapidly down nearby valleys and burying fields, settlements and people. Almost the entire population of Armero in Ecuador was killed by such a mudflow in November 1985 (**D**). Mudflows can also be caused by the water which collects in crater lakes while the volcanoes are dormant.

Tidal Waves (Tsunamis) Eruptions beneath the ocean or on volcanic islands can produce tidal waves a long way from the original site. The most famous case in recent times was the eruption of Krakatoa in 1883. When the volcanic island exploded, over 36,000 people were swept to their deaths along the coasts of Java and Sumatra by waves up to 35 metres high. 300 towns and villages were destroyed.

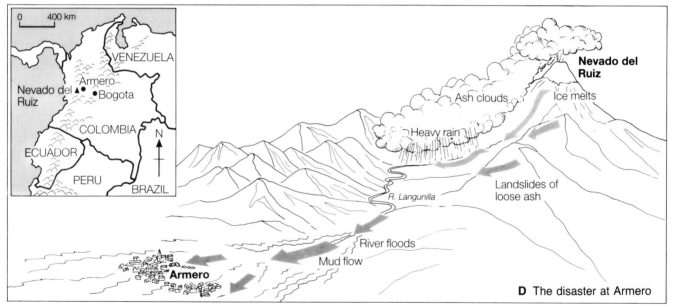

D The disaster at Armero

1 Write a sentence explaining each of these terms:
  a nuée ardente, b lava bomb, c tsunami, d flash flood.
2 a Look at A. Which country on the list seems to suffer from the greatest loss of life? Why is this?
  b Most of the disasters in A are located around the Pacific Ocean. Why?
  c Why does the death toll vary so much between disasters?
3 a Make a list of the ways in which volcanic eruptions can lead to disasters.

b Which of the effects you have listed in **a** are most likely to result in a high death toll? Explain your answer.
4 Study D.
  a Draw a flow diagram to show the causes of the Armero disaster.
  b Imagine you are a local newspaper reporter. Write an article describing the causes and effects of the Armero disaster.
  c The people of Armero were given some warning of a volcanic eruption. Why were they unwilling to move away from the town?

6 : The Eruption of Mount St Helens

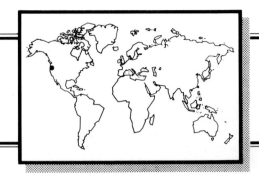

MOUNT ST HELENS is one of 15 major volcanoes in the Cascade Range of western N. America (see **E**). The Cascades are part of 'The Ring of Fire' which surrounds the Pacific Ocean. They lie to the east of a **subduction zone** where the small Juan de Fuca plate pushes under the North American plate.

Most of the Cascade volcanoes have erupted during the last 1000 years. Mount St Helens was last active between 1831 and 1857. Studies by geologists showed that it had erupted at least 20 times in the past 4500 years.

The Eruption of 18 May 1980

Mount St Helens was considered dormant until 1980, but it was known to have produced dangerous explosive activity during its occasional eruptions. The first sign of renewed activity was an earthquake under the mountain on 20 March. Swarms of local earthquakes, then small eruptions of steam and ash followed. The earthquakes suggested that magma was moving deep underground. Large cracks appeared in the cap of snow and ice.

As clouds of steam and ash rose above the summit, other signs of an imminent eruption appeared. The main crater became deeper and wider and a bulge appeared on the north side of the cone. This bulge was growing outwards by about 1.5m per day (**D**).

At 8.32 am on 18 May the mountain was shaken by an earthquake centred below its northern flank. Seconds later, a huge avalanche of rock, soil, snow and ice slid down the north side of the volcano. More than 2 cubic kilometres of material was deposited into Spirit Lake and the Toutle River at velocities as high as 250 km/hr.

Almost immediately, this avalanche released the pressure within the cone. Superheated steam and gases from the magma exploded from the north side of the volcano to form a dense, debris-filled cloud (nuée ardente) which billowed down the slope at up to 400 km/hr. The cloud hugged the

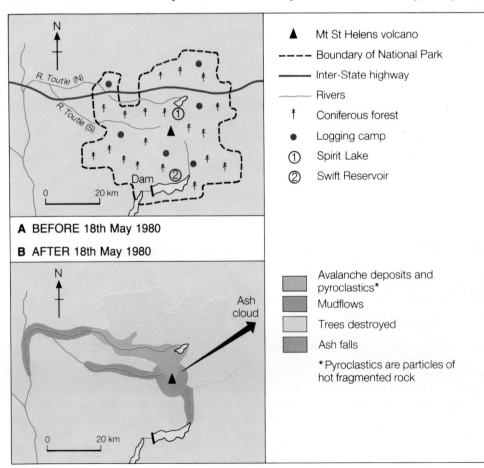

Key:

▲ Mt St Helens volcano
--- Boundary of National Park
— Inter-State highway
— Rivers
↑ Coniferous forest
● Logging camp
① Spirit Lake
② Swift Reservoir

A BEFORE 18th May 1980

B AFTER 18th May 1980

Avalanche deposits and pyroclastics*
Mudflows
Trees destroyed
Ash falls

*Pyroclastics are particles of hot fragmented rock

C The eruption of Mt. St Helens

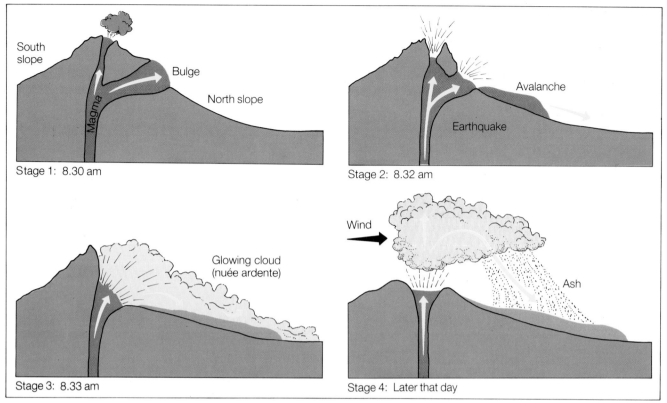

South slope

Magma

Bulge

North slope

Stage 1: 8.30 am

Avalanche

Earthquake

Stage 2: 8.32 am

Glowing cloud
(nuée ardente)

Stage 3: 8.33 am

Wind

Ash

Stage 4: Later that day

D Stages in the eruption of Mount St Helens, 18 May 1980

ground, destroying trees over an area of 550 square kilometres to the north of the mountain. On the edge of the zone of destruction, the trees were still standing but their needles were scorched beyond recovery (**B**).

By 9 am the worst of the eruption was over, but a new hazard had appeared. A great column of ash rose more than 20 km above the new crater. Winds from the south west carried the ash towards towns hundreds of kilometres away, leaving deposits more than 7 cm deep over crops, roads and houses, and blocking out the sun. Within three days, the fine ash had crossed the USA.

On the slopes to the north of the volcano, the ash mixed with melting snow and ice, with condensed steam and with water from Spirit Lake and the Toutle River to produce mudflows (**B**). These blocked the rivers and lakes, covered fields and destroyed the state fishing hatchery. The final death toll was 60 people. 20 bodies were never found, including scientists, local residents and tourists.

1 Why was the death toll on 18 May 1980 so low? Give as many reasons as you can.
2 What evidence was there before 1980 that Mount St Helens would erupt again?
3 What evidence was there just before 18 May 1980 that the volcano would soon erupt?
4 Describe the types of disaster which could affect the landscape and the local economy if Mount St Helens erupted. Use evidence from **A** and **B**.
5 Name two groups of people in the Mount St Helens area who might not leave despite warnings of a possible volcanic eruption. In each case give one reason why.

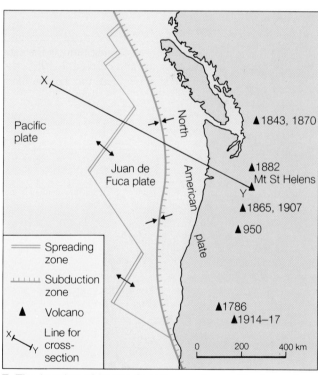

Pacific
plate

Juan de
Fuca plate

North

American

plate

▲1843, 1870

▲1882
Mt St Helens
▲

▲1865, 1907

▲950

▲1786
▲1914–17

════ Spreading zone
⊥⊥⊥⊥ Subduction zone
▲ Volcano
X—Y Line for cross-section

0   200   400 km

E The location of Mount St Helens volcano. Numbers show dates of previous volcanic eruptions

6 Study **E** which shows plate margins in the north west Pacific and part of western North America.
   a Draw and label fully a sketch section from **X** to **Y** along the line indicated.
   b Briefly explain why there are active volcanoes in this part of North America.

15

7 : Living with Volcanoes

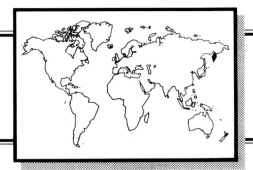

Cutting Your Losses   Although volcanic eruptions can-not be prevented, some measures can be taken to reduce their effects on human activity.

1   The people who live near Etna remove the doors, windows and roof tiles from their homes before they are bulldozed by advancing lava. They may then be re-used, which cuts the costs of building a new house.

2   During the eruption of Heimaey in Iceland in 1973, a lava flow was sprayed with millions of litres of sea water so that it became cooler and less fluid. In this way, the rate of flow of the lava was reduced.

3   In 1983, lava from Etna was partly diverted by digging a trench and using dynamite to blow a hole through the wall of the lava channel.

4   Lava flows in Hawaii have been bombed in partly successful attempts to breach the natural levees (embankments) which build up at the side of flowing lava.

5   To prevent a repeat of the 1919 disaster, the crater lake at Kelut in Java was drained by digging tunnels through the crater wall. When the volcano erupted in 1951, the lake was so small that it evaporated and no mudflow resulted.

HEAT ON TAP

A 200-MEGAWATT power station harnessing the earth's own natural heat is to be built in a geyser valley on trhe Kamchatka Peninsula in the Soviet Far East.

It will be the second geothermal station in the area, says the Soviet Power Engineering and Elect-rification Ministry. The first, the eleven-megawatt Pauzhetskaya station, was built a dozen years ago.

Though small, the experience gained through the experimental project is now being applied in designing similar power stations for various parts of the USSR.

The new station will use water heated to 200 degrees Celsius by the nearby Mutnovsky volcano nearly a kilometre underground.

Experts reckon the station will meet all the peninsula's hot water and power needs, both industrial and domestic.

Hot water will be piped to Petropavlovsk-Kamchatsky and other towns, and will save around 400,000 tons of fuel each year.

Guidelines for the long-term economic development of the country attach great importance to stations relying on renewable power sources and several geothermal power stations are to be built in the northern Caucasus and the Ukraine.

B *Source:* Soviet Weekly

The Benefits Of Volcanic Activity

The most sensible precaution against a disaster would seem to be to evacuate everyone living near an active volcano. However, volcanic areas can be very beneficial to humans.

- **Soils**   Some of the most fertile soils in the world form from volcanic rocks. Under hot, moist climatic condi-tions the rocks weather rapidly. This releases the minerals needed for rich harvests of rice and other tropical crops. These soils are capable of producing several crops a year with very high yields per hectare. They also support the highest rural population densi-ties in the world. For example, the small island of Java feeds a population of 100 million, double the popula-tion of the entire United Kingdom.

- **Rocks and Minerals**   Minerals are found in volcanic rocks or around vents where hot gases and water seep from underground. The minerals found in volcanic regions include sulphur and borax, which are used to make products such as cement, glass, gunpowder and drugs.

  Metals such as iron, copper, nickel, manganese and arsenic, occur in some volcanic regions. Hardened lava is used as building stone, in road building, or as an abrasive.

![Map of the 1973 Heimaey eruption showing the island of Heimaey with scale 0 to 2 km, north arrow, Atlantic Ocean. Legend: New cone (Kirkefell), Old cone (Helgafell), New lava flow, Area of ash fall, Town, Airfield.]

0   2 km   N

HEIMAEY

ATLANTIC   OCEAN

New cone (Kirkefell)
Old cone (Helgafell)
New lava flow
Area of ash fall
Town
Airfield

Fig. A The 1973 Heimaey eruption

- **Geothermal Energy**   Some of the cheapest electricity in the world is generated by steam derived from hot springs. Such heat energy from beneath the Earth's surface is called **geothermal**. It produces about 10% of New Zealand's power supply (**C**), and is also important in Italy and California. The people of Iceland find it particularly useful for heating houses, swimming pools, factories and greenhouses, as well as underground heating in fields.
- **Tourism**   Hot water fountains or **geysers**, such as Old Faithful in Yellowstone National Park, USA, are a major attraction for tourists. Spectacular scenery and snow-capped peaks provide ideal sites for skiers and holidaymakers. Hotels near Etna and Kilauea are packed with tourists during their frequent eruptions.
- **Communications**   Volcanic islands are often found in mid-ocean, so they can provide useful stopping off places on long air or sea journeys. Examples are Ascension Island and the Canary Islands, both in the Atlantic Ocean.

C Weiraki Thermal Power Station, New Zealand

1   Study the map of Heimaey (**A**) then answer these questions:
   a What was the name of the active volcanic cone?
   b What was the greatest distance at which ash fell from the active volcanic cone?
   c Why was it necessary to evacuate 6000 people from the town?
   d Why was no-one killed by lava before the evacuation was completed?
   e Why were the local fishermen happy about the new lava flow?
   f What work needed to be done before the island could be re-occupied?

2   Study **B**, a newspaper article from Soviet Weekly.
   a What is geothermal energy?
   b What is the geothermal energy used for?
   c Use an atlas to find the places mentioned in the article. Suggest why this geothermal scheme is so important to the Kamchatka Peninsula.
   d Where else in the USSR is geothermal energy going to be used?
   e With the aid of an atlas, suggest why geothermal energy is likely to be less important to the USSR than to New Zealand or Iceland.

3   Look at **D**.
   a What human activities are shown?
   b Explain why the human activity in the area is so well developed.
   c Make a list of the possible consequences of an eruption for the area shown.

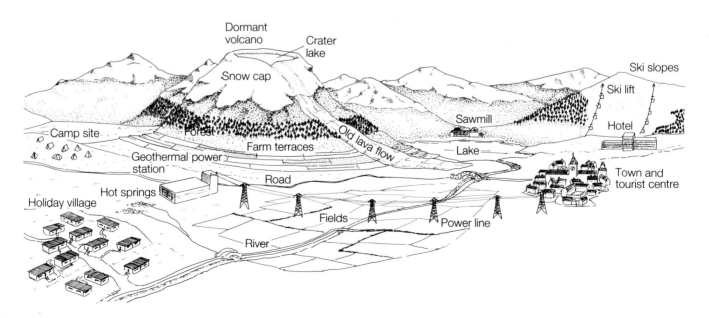

D Development of a volcanic region

8 : Earthquakes

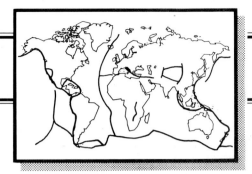

AN EARTHQUAKE IS a tremor or vibration of the Earth's crust. More than 150,000 earthquakes happen every year. Most tremors are so small that they cannot be felt by humans, though they can be detected by sensitive instruments called **seismometers**. Between 20 and 100 earthquakes each year cause damage to roads, bridges and buildings, and result in loss of life.

Major earthquakes release huge amounts of energy, equivalent to a large nuclear explosion, within a few minutes. The destructive power of an earthquake is measured by the amount of energy it releases. This is shown by the Richter Scale. An increase of one whole number on this scale means that an earthquake releases 30 times more energy. A magnitude 8 earthquake releases about 800,000 times as much energy as a magnitude 4 earthquake. The most powerful earthquakes ever recorded have been at 8.9 on the Richter Scale.

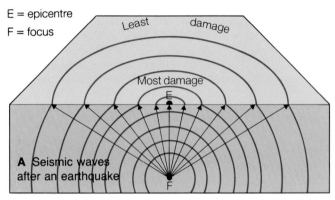

E = epicentre
F = focus

A Seismic waves after an earthquake

The place where the earthquake originates is called its **focus** (A). Shock waves spread out from the focus in all directions, like ripples on a pool, but the maximum destruction of lives and property usually occurs at the **epicentre** directly above the focus. The amount of damage usually decreases with distance from the epicentre. However, soft sediments can shake like jelly and cause heavy damage far from the epicentre, as happened in Mexico City in 1985 (**E**).

The Richter Scale and Typical Effects

1
2 } Detected only by seismometers.

3 Felt only by sensitive people. Slight vibrations like those from a passing vehicle.

4 Moderate vibration, movement of loose objects.

5 Strong vibration. People frightened. Windows shatter. Objects fall off shelves.

6 Damage to buildings. Chimneys fall. Walls crack.

7 Disaster. Ground cracks. Pipes break. Buildngs collapse. Possible landslides.

8 Total destruction. Ground moves up and down in waves. Cracks open and close. Dams damaged. Towns destroyed. Major landslides.

The Causes of Earthquakes   Most major earthquakes are related to great fractures in the crust called **faults**. When the crust is under stress, it will bend, producing folds in the rock. However, if the stress continues, the crust can suddenly break. A sudden jerking movement of the crust on either side of a fault, whether up or down or sideways, will cause an earthquake (**B**). Some fault movements, such as those along transform faults, produce shallow-focus earthquakes only 15–20 km below the surface. Other earthquakes can take place at much greater depths, perhaps hundreds of kilometres underground.

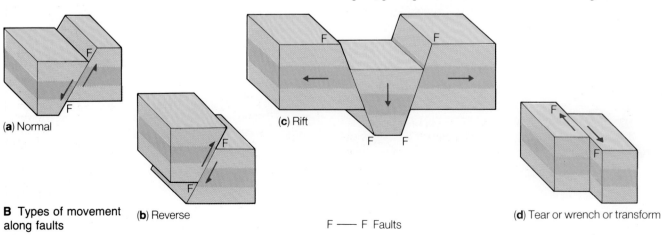

(a) Normal

(b) Reverse

(c) Rift

(d) Tear or wrench or transform

B Types of movement along faults

F —— F Faults

18

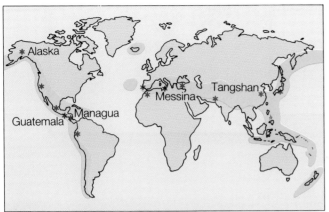

*   Sites of major earthquake disasters

  Major earthquake zones

C The world's main Earthquake zones

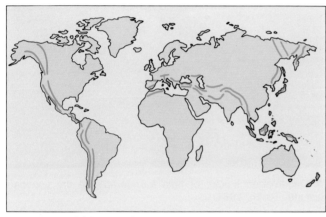

‿   Young fold mountains

D The world's young fold mountains

E The 1985 earthquake in Mexico City

1 Write a sentence explaining the meaning of each of these terms:
    a focus **b** epicentre **c** fault **d** Richter scale.

2 **B** shows the types of crustal movement along faults. Briefly explain what happens in each case.

3 Study the summary of the Richter Scale on page 17. Draw and label a series of seven diagrams to show the effects of different magnitudes of earthquake.

4 Study **A**, then explain why 'the amount of damage usually decreases with distance from the epicentre'.

5 **a** On an outline map of the world, mark in the main earthquake zones shown in **C**.
    b Mark on your outline map the location of the major earthquake disasters listed in **F**, and label them.
    c Explain the location of earthquakes
    • around the shores of the Pacific Ocean,
    • in the belt from China to the Mediterranean,
    • in Iceland. Use **D**, and **A** on p8 to help you.

The Distribution of Earthquakes Faults occur nearly everywhere in the crust, but many are no longer active, like those in Britain. Others allow a slow, continuous creep of the rocks on either side of a fault.

A map of world earthquakes shows that they are nearly all found close to plate boundaries (**C**). Shallow-focus earthquakes are concentrated along ocean ridges (see unit 3). Most of these are weak and far from land, so they offer little threat.

Other, more serious, quakes occur every few decades along transform faults or tear faults (**B**). The longer the plates lock in position, the more damaging will be the quake that follows.

Most of the earthquakes which cause loss of life every year take place near plate collision zones. Examples are

* a **subduction zone** close to an ocean trench, eg the west coast of South America. Here the oceanic plate is bending and being forced down beneath the continental plate. The result is a zone of deeper focus earthquakes all around the edge of the Pacific Ocean.
* a **continental collision zone**, eg the Mediterranean Sea or the Himalayas . Here two continental plates are moving towards each other, creating fold mountains (**D**) and fractures in the crust.

F Some major earthquake disasters

Date	Earthquake	Deaths
1556	Shensi, China	830,000
1755	Lisbon, Portugal	60,000
1906	San Francisco, USA	700
1923	Tokyo, Japan	156,000
1935	Quetta, Pakistan	60,000
1939	Erzincan, Turkey	40,000
1960	Agadir, Morocco	14,000
1964	Anchorage, Alaska	115
1970	Yungay, Peru	30,000
1972	Managua, Nicaragua	12,000
1976	Guatemala City, Guatemala	23,000
1976	Tangshan, China	500,000+
1985	Mexico City, Mexico	10,000

9 : The Effects of Earthquakes

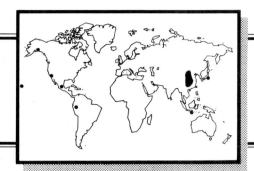

SEVERE EARTHQUAKES occur in some of the most densely-populated parts of the world, such as Japan and China. The loss of life and cost of damage is very high in such areas, especially if there are large settlements near the epicentre.

Collapsing buildings and bridges account for most loss of life during earthquakes. Buildings are particularly vulnerable if they are built on soft sediments such as alluvium. The ground turns into quicksand so that buildings tip on end and sink into the ground . Soft sediments also shake more than solid rock (**A**).

People may be trapped beneath piles of rubble or killed by flying debris in the street. Hospitals and other emergency services may be hit, so that people die from exposure to the weather, from lack of food and water, or from disease. Fallen bridges, twisted rail tracks, damaged roads and airfields all slow down the arrival of help from outside.

There are other hazards. Fire often results when gas and oil pipes and storage tanks break under the strain. Water pipes are also destroyed, and without a water supply, fire-fighting is affected. This was a major problem in San Francisco in 1906 and Tokyo in 1923. Dams may burst, releasing huge volumes of water in catastrophic floods. One possible hazard which has not yet occurred (1988) is the destruction of nuclear installations with release of radioactivity into the atmosphere.

Many earthquakes occur in mountainous country. Loose snow, ice and rock on the steep slopes can easily be dislodged. This happened in the Peruvian earthquake of 1970. The shock caused the ice cap of Mt Huascaran to break free, triggering an avalanche. As the snow and ice rushed downhill it picked up loose rocks up to 15m across and turned into a giant mudflow, travelling at a speed of over

A Undamaged blocks of flats foundered into the liquefied ground, Japan, 1964

320 km/hour. The debris covered the Shacsha Valley and the town of Yungay to a depth of 80m. Only 92 of the town's 25,000 inhabitants escaped, by running to higher ground.

Tsunamis (wrongly called tidal waves) are giant ocean waves created by sudden movements of the ocean floor. They can be volcanic in origin (eg the Krakatoa eruption of 1883), or they may be seismic. A series of waves spreads out from the epicentre at speeds of up to 750 km/hour. In the open ocean, the waves pass unnoticed, but when they reach the coast, the water piles up into waves 12m or more high (**B**).

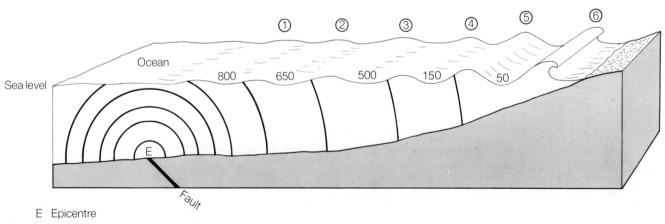

E   Epicentre
①-⑥   Series of waves
800   Speed in km/h

B Growth of Tsunamis

After the 1964 Alaskan earthquake, tsunamis up to 7m high flooded 30 blocks, caused damage estimated at $7m and killed ten people in Crescent City, California, thousands of kilometres from the epicentre (**C**). The people who were killed had returned to clean up after the first waves and were drowned when the giant third and fourth waves hit the city.

Many lives have been saved by the Tsunami Warning System. This was set up in Honolulu in 1946 after a tsunami drowned many people in Hawaii following an earthquake off the Aleutian Islands. Warnings of possible tsunamis are now sent to all countries around the Pacific Ocean.

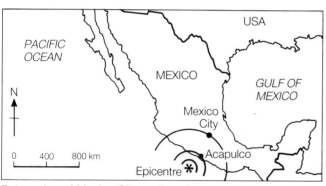

C The spread of the Alaskan Tsunamis, 1964

1 **a** What are the two main causes of tsunamis? (see also unit 5)
b The common name given to a tsunami is 'tidal wave'. Why is this common name incorrect?
c Study **D**. Why was there the fear of tsunamis after the Mexico City earthquake disaster of 1985?
d Study **B**. Explain why tsunamis are only noticed by ships near the coast.
e How many hours did it take the Alaskan tsunamis to reach Crescent City in 1964? If Crescent City is 2800 km from the epicentre, what was the average speed at which the tsunamis travelled?

2 Explain why the worst damage in the 1985 Mexico City earthquake was to buildings located on an old lake bed.

3 Complete the table below, using the words HIGH, MODERATE or LOW.

Earthquake Effect	Property Damage	Deaths
Ground shaking (urban area)		
Ground shaking (rural area)		
Faulting (urban area)		
Faulting (rural area)		
Tsunami (coastal city)		
Tsunami (coastal rice padi)		
Landslide/ avalanche		

D Location of Mexico City earthquake

4 Copy the diagram below (**E**), and complete the labels.

E Earthquake Hazards

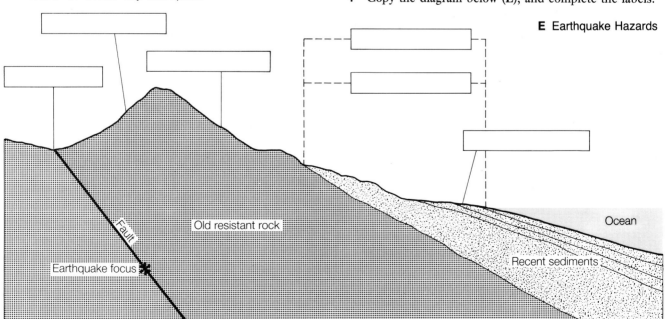

Old resistant rock

Fault

Earthquake focus

Ocean

Recent sediments

21

10 : Reducing the Impact of Earthquakes

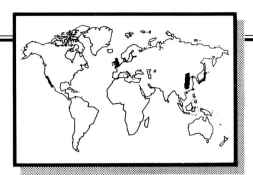

EARLY WARNING of earthquakes could save thousands of lives. Unfortunately, when millions of people have to be evacuated, false alarms can be very costly. Earthquake prediction is not yet very advanced, although some signs have been recognised:

- the rocks swell as small cracks open up in them;
- radon gas is released from cracked rocks into the ground and soil;
- water levels in wells may rise or fall;
- animals may act strangely;
- weak foreshocks may be recorded by seismometers;
- long periods with little seismic activity;
- lights may appear in the sky, either a broad glow or sudden flashes.

Batteries of instruments are used to measure these effects in places like California (A), but not every country has the scientists or money for such intensive studies. The Chinese make up for their lack of technology by using large numbers of investigators. Their greatest success was in 1975, when they correctly forecast a major earthquake near Haicheng after a period of strange animal behaviour and some minor tremors. When the quake came, more than one million people were safely camping out in parks and fields. Only about 300 died instead of many thousands.

Unfortunately, human activity can increase the likelihood of earthquakes. In the 1960's it was discovered that water pumped into the ground near fault lines in the USA and Japan set off a series of earthquakes. It was already

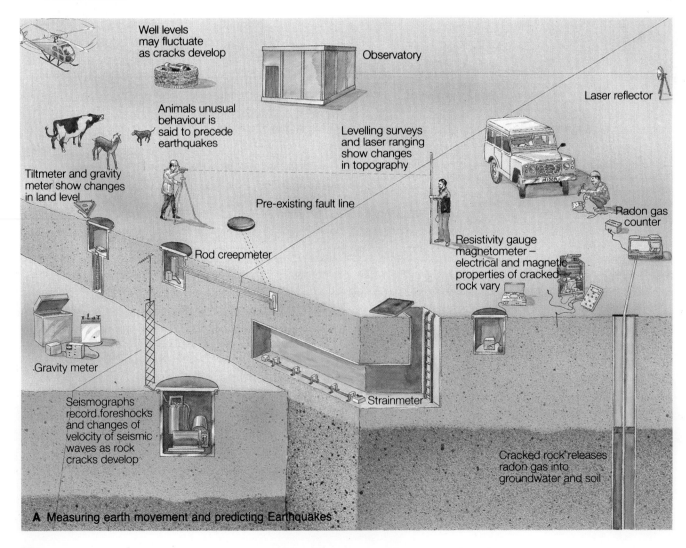

A Measuring earth movement and predicting Earthquakes

B How to build safer skyscrapers. The Trans-American Building in San Francisco, California

1 Draw a series of simple diagrams to show the possible warning signs that an earthquake may soon occur.
2 Study **A**.
  a Name five instruments which enable us to measure movement in the crust.
  b For each instrument you have named in **a**, explain the way it works.
3 **a** What types of buildings have been found to be most vulnerable during earthquakes?
  b Study **B**. Suggest why this method of construction is safer.
  c Why are deaths caused by collapsed buildings during earthquakes less likely in developed countries?
4 Study **C**.
  a What magnitude are most British earthquakes?
  b What magnitude are the most powerful earthquakes in Britain?
  c Which parts of Britain seem to have a stable crust?
  d Do you agree that all new buildings in Britain should be earthquake-proof, and that everyone should be educated in earthquake emergency procedures? Give reasons for your answer.
5 **a** Imagine you are the mayor of a large city. Scientists have predicted that there will be a major earthquake nearby in the next few months. Write a list of all the emergency measures you would introduce in order to reduce loss of life and damage to property.
  b Explain the reasons for each emergency measure.

known that large reservoirs behind dams could trigger swarms of tremors along inactive faults. The water acted as a lubricant, causing old, inactive faults to slip. This suggests that stress could be gradually released by pumping water underground along faults. In places like California, where major earthquakes are a threat, this is a tempting idea, but a risky one.

Safety Precautions

Until some way is found of preventing major earthquakes, the only answer is to erect safer buildings. Most loss of life and property is due to the collapse of old or unsafe buildings. The problem is to design structures which can withstand severe horizontal and vertical motions.

Offices raised on columns and sheathed in glass were tested on shaking tables and found to be death traps. Instead, walls made of triangular steel or concrete frames were found to absorb huge amounts of stress. Reinforced brick and concrete houses are replacing traditional designs in wood, mud or brick in many parts of the world (**B**).

Before the 1964 Alaskan earthquake, major electricity generators were equipped with shutdown switches activated by the earthquake. The major gas mains were also automatically shut off by sudden pressure changes. This meant a great reduction in fire damage after the earthquake.

In Japan, a Large-Scale Earthquake Countermeasures Act was passed in 1980. Billions of dollars are being spent on preparations for Tokyo's next big quake:
- wooden houses are being replaced by concrete apartments;
- a 10 day supply of drinking water has been stored in underground cisterns and quakeproof warehouses;
- evacuation routes are being expanded;
- bridges and public buildings are being reinforced;
- earthquake drills are practised regularly;
- each district has its disaster plan and civil defence group;
- survival kits are found in many homes;
- food, blankets and babies' bottles are stockpiled throughout the city.

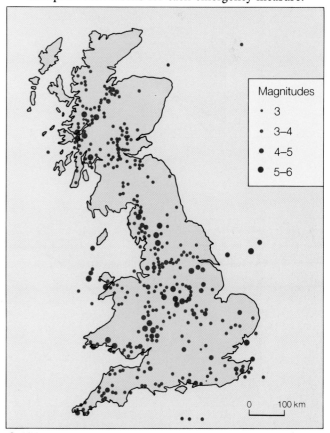

C UK earthquake epicentres with size inferred from historical records c 1000 AD to present

11 : Weathering and Erosion

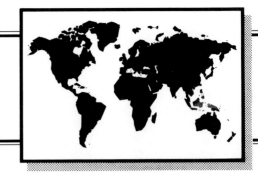

IN THE DISTANT past, the mountains of Britain were as tall as the Alps, up to 4,800 metres. Today the highest peak only rises to 1,344 metres above sea level. The summits have worn away over the last 400 million years.

Even the hardest rocks can be broken down into smaller pieces by rain, frost and changes in temperature. This process is known as **weathering**. The weathering process is helped by lines of weakness in rocks such as the **bedding planes** found between layers in sedimentary rocks or the natural cracks called **joints** which occur in rocks such as granite and limestone.

There are three main types of weathering: mechanical, chemical, and biological.

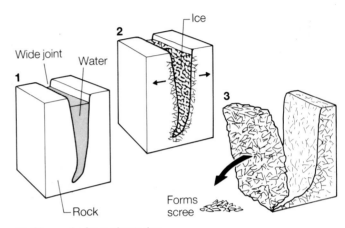

B Stages in frost shattering

Mechanical weathering occurs when a rock is broken up by a force acting upon it. This is usually caused by extreme temperature changes. **Frost shattering** is found in regions where temperatures plunge below freezing. It occurs when water trapped in cracks freezes and expands, forcing the rock to split (**B**). A sign of this process is seen in **screes**, loose fragments, rocks and boulders covering the slopes of a mountain (**E**).

A second type of mechanical weathering is known as **exfoliation**. This is found in desert areas where there is a wide daily temperature range. During the day the ground surface may reach over 40°C, but at night can fall to freezing. The surface of the rock is heated and cooled more than the centre, and tends to flake off in layers, like an onion (**C**). The flaking is also helped by the formation of salt crystals as water evaporates from the rock surface.

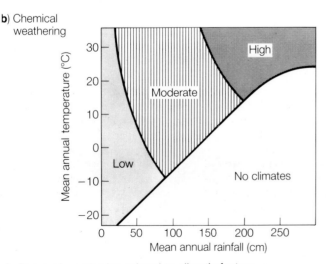

(**a**) Mechanical weathering

(**b**) Chemical weathering

A Rates of weathering related to climatic factors

C Weathering in the Australian Desert

Chemical weathering is caused by rainwater and gases in the atmosphere. Rainwater is naturally slightly acid as it carries dissolved carbon dioxide from the atmosphere. This **carbonic acid** in normal rain reacts with minerals in rocks. Rain (carbonic acid) and calcium carbonate (the main ingredient of chalk and limestone) react to produce calcium bicarbonate which can be easily washed away (**D** and **F**). Felspar, a mineral found in granite, reacts to produce a soft clay. Oxygen in the atmosphere can also react with minerals like iron to produce the crumbly iron oxide known as rust. Note that **acid rain** (see unit 49) is different from normal, slightly acidic, rain.

Formation of carbonic acid in rainwater

CO_2	$+ H_2O$	$\rightarrow H_2CO_3$
Carbon dioxide in atmosphere	Pure rain water	Carbonic acid rainwater

Chemical weathering of chalk and limestone

H_2CO_3	$+ CaCO_3$	$\rightarrow Ca(HCO_3)_2$
Carbonic acid rainwater	Chalk or limestone (calcium carbonate)	Calcium bicarbonate (soluble)

D Chemical reactions involving rainwater

Biological weathering is caused by the action of plants or plant matter on rocks. Roots of plants can penetrate into rock joints, and help to break up the rock. Dead plant matter produces acids as it decays, and these can also attack rock minerals.

Over a long period, weathering creates a waste mantle which turns into soil. In humid tropical regions, weathering is so rapid that soils up to 100 metres thick are formed.

All loose weathered material is removed by agents of **transportation** such as running water, glacier ice and wind. These agents can also wear down rocks by themselves or when the material they carry rubs against the exposed rock. This wearing down of the surface through movement is called **erosion**.

E Weathering in the Yorkshire Dales

F Limestone pavement in Yorkshire

1 Copy and complete these sentences by adding the correct word in the spaces:
   a The breakdown of a rock by elements of weather is called . . . .
   b Mechanical weathering involves action on rock by a physical . . . . .
   c Chemical weathering involves rotting of minerals by slightly . . . . rainwater.
   d Chalk is weathered when calcium carbonate reacts with . . . .
   e Exfoliation takes place when rock surfaces are subjected to extreme . . . .

2 Put these agents under the correct headings (either **Weathering**, **Transport** or **Erosion**). Wind, waves, glacier, frost, human trampling, strong heating, rain, tree roots.

3 Copy **B**. Then briefly explain what is happening in each of the three stages.

4 **a** Study **C**, **E**, and **F**. Describe what each picture shows, then suggest which type of weathering it represents.
   b Explain why bishops, houseowners and architects see weathering as an expensive problem, and farmers see it as a blessing.

5 Study **A**.
   a Which parts of the world experience the most rapid mechanical weathering? Explain your answer.
   b What conditions of temperature and rainfall result in the most rapid chemical weathering?
   c Which regions of the world experience the most rapid chemical weathering?
   d What are the rates of mechanical and chemical weathering in Britain? Explain your answer.

12 : The Sliding Land

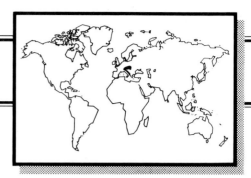

MOST OF THE WORLD'S land surface is not flat. When thick layers of loose weathered material build up on hill slopes, they may begin to move downhill – a process known as **mass movement**. As the name **soil creep** suggests, this movement is usually very slow in countries with temperate climates such as Britain (**A**).

It is much more dangerous when large volumes of material on steep slopes suddenly start moving. These movements are called landslides, avalanches, rock falls or mudflows according to their exact nature, but they have several features in common:

- they take place on steep slopes under the influence of gravity.
- they involve large volumes of loose material such as snow, rock, soil.
- they are often triggered by a natural event such as an earthquake or rainstorm.
- water within the loose material adds to its weight and also reduces friction between particles or boulders.
- there are devastating secondary effects. Rivers may be blocked or diverted, causing floods and the formation of new lakes. Material entering lakes or reservoirs creates giant waves.

Avalanches

The most serious avalanches occur in temperate regions, such as the Alps of Switzerland, Austria and northern Italy. Winters there are long, snow collects at lower altitudes, and valleys are densely-populated. Many of those killed or injured by avalanches are tourists, who are less aware of the dangers than local people.

What Causes Avalanches? Tens of thousands of avalanches occur in the Alps every year between the first snows of late November and the slow thaw of April to June. Avalanches can be triggered by a sudden thaw, a loud noise, an earthquake or just a build up of too much snow. However, there are some factors which play an important part in most avalanches:

- a considerable depth of snow in different layers.
- a lack of bonding or strength in the ice crystals due to melting during warm spells or in spring.
- slope gradient – the steeper the slope, the more likely an avalanche.
- lack of ground cover – trees and bushes tend to bind the snow.

A Some features of slow mass movement

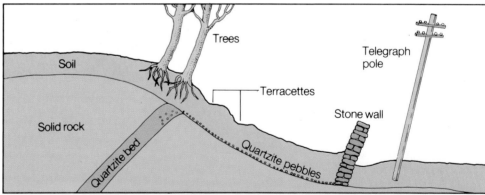

B Three types of sudden mass movement

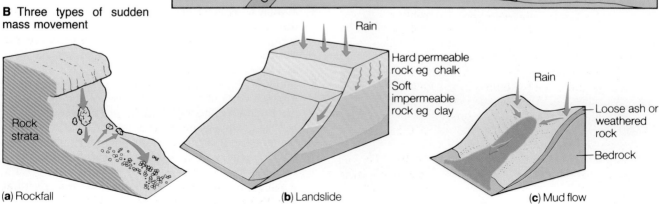

(**a**) Rockfall

(**b**) Landslide

(**c**) Mud flow

26

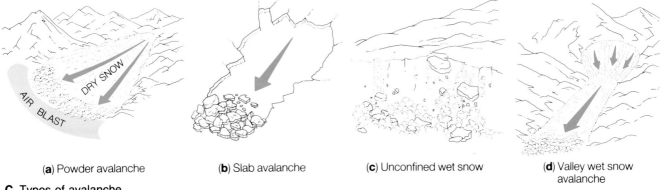

(a) Powder avalanche (b) Slab avalanche (c) Unconfined wet snow (d) Valley wet snow avalanche

C Types of avalanche

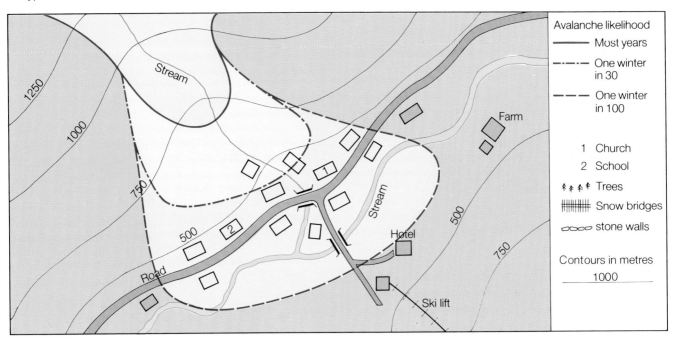

D Avalanche hazard map

Various efforts have been made to reduce the likelihood of disasters.

- Observation and monitoring stations enable advance warning to be broadcast. Risk maps can be drawn to show areas most in danger (**D**).
- Barriers are built on bare, exposed slopes above the tree line (the upper limit of tree growth) or along the routes most commonly taken by the avalanches.

  The upper barriers, made of wood, aluminium or steel, are intended to prevent the first slip of snow and ice. Terraces can also be cut into the hillside. Snow fences can be erected to deflect the wind and prevent drifting of snow. Lower down, stone walls are built to break up the slide or guide it away from buildings.
- Buildings may be strengthened and ramps added to deflect the force of the avalanche. Road and rail routes may be protected by tunnels in risk areas.
- The spread of Alpine cattle pastures has caused the tree line to be lowered. To offset this, thousands of trees are being planted in the zones most likely to breed avalanches.
- Small avalanches can be triggered before the full weight of the snow and ice has developed into a much bigger threat. This is done by mortar shells or hand-held charges.

1 **a** What is meant by mass movement?
  b Study **A**. What evidence in the diagram suggests that mass movement is taking place?
2 **a** Study **B**. Describe and explain the differences between the three types of mass movement shown.
  b Study **C**. Describe and explain the differences between the four types of avalanche shown.
3 Look at an atlas map of Switzerland. Give three reasons why Switzerland suffers more deaths and property damage from avalanches than any other European country.
4 Trace or draw a copy of **D**.
  a Suggest three reasons why the village was first located there.
  b Colour in red the FIVE buildings you consider most at risk. Give a reason for your choice.
  c Imagine you are on the village council. Add to your map any avalanche defences you would propose to the other councillors (eg tree plantations, snow bridges, stone guide walls etc). Use the symbols provided in the key. Explain the reasons for your choices.

27

13 : Living in the Mountains

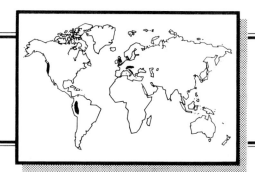

ALL OF THE CONTINENTS contain mountain ranges which reach altitudes of more than 2,500 metres (unit 8 **D**). The very highest mountains are not suitable for permanent human settlement because the gradient is too steep, the air is too thin to breathe, temperatures are too low, and there are permanent caps of ice and snow. Lower altitudes, particularly valley bottoms, are more suitable for human activity.

Climate Mountains are usually very wet places. When air is forced to rise over mountains, it expands and cools. Any water vapour in the air condenses to form clouds. These dense clouds over mountains produce **relief rain** or snow. When the air sinks down the other side of the mountains, it gets warmer, so the clouds thin or disappear (**A**). This area therefore has lower rainfall and is known as a **rain shadow**.

Thin, clear mountain air is unable to absorb much heat, even on the sunniest of days. Temperatures decrease on average about 0.6°C for every 100 metres higher up you go. They are also affected by **aspect**. Slopes with a south-facing aspect (in the northern hemisphere) receive much more solar radiation than north-facing slopes, which are often in shadow and therefore much colder. Snow lies much longer on north-facing slopes.

Natural Vegetation As climate changes with altitude, so the natural vegetation also changes. There are many variations (**B**), but the densest forest vegetation is usually found on lower slopes where temperatures are warmer, soil is deeper, and land is sheltered. Above the **tree line** (the level above which trees cannot survive), grass provides pasture for wild or domesticated animals. Above the **snow line** there is permanent snow and ice. Vegetation zones are lower on northern slopes.

Human Activity

Mountains are most densely populated in tropical regions where sea-level temperatures average 30°C or more. Above the warm, wet tropical rainforest of the lower slopes, there is a more pleasant temperate climate. This enables plantation crops such as coffee, and food crops such as wheat, barley and potatoes to be grown where there is sufficient soil and flat land. Where flat land is scarce, people build terraces, often with their bare hands. The highest cities in the world are found on the fertile Andean plateau more than 3,000 m above sea level. Only on the highest slopes in tropical regions is the land too cold and barren for human use.

In the cooler lands of mid-latitude, only the valley floors are permanently settled. Towns and villages grow along the road and rail routes which follow the winding valleys. Mixed farms are common, with cereals, cattle or sheep, and fodder crops for the livestock to eat when they are brought indoors. Winter snowfall closes many mountain passes.

Transhumance is widely found in mountains. Livestock farmers move their animals to the high 'alpine' pastures when the snow melts in summer. The animals (and sometimes the farmers) stay on these pastures until early autumn, producing butter and cheese and cutting grass for hay. This is very important since farms are often small and land available for fodder crops is limited.

A Relief rain

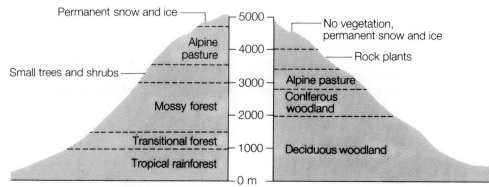

B Vegetation zones in the Andes and Alps

28

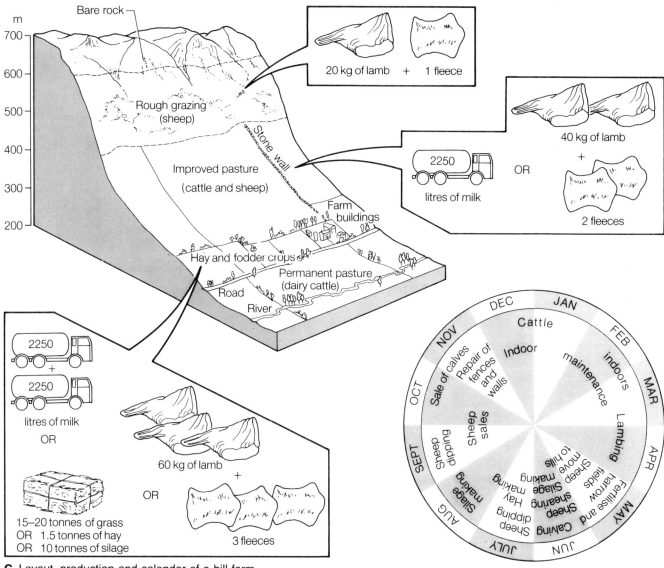

20 kg of lamb + 1 fleece

2250 litres of milk OR 40 kg of lamb + 2 fleeces

2250 litres of milk + 2250 litres of milk OR 15–20 tonnes of grass OR 1.5 tonnes of hay OR 10 tonnes of silage OR 60 kg of lamb OR 3 fleeces

C Layout, production and calendar of a hill farm

D An alpine valley

Transhumance in July
– – – ⟶

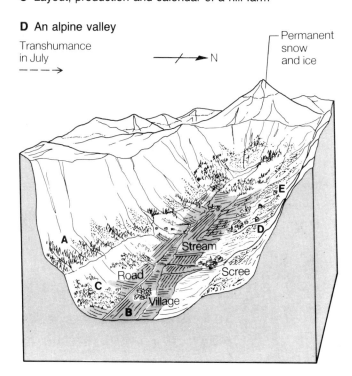

1 Write a sentence explaining the meaning of each of these terms:
   a tree line **b** snow line **c** glacier **d** aspect.

2 Study **A**. Write a brief explanation of stages 1–4 in the formation of relief rain.

3 **a** What are the differences between the vegetation zones in the Andes and the Alps?
   b Explain why these vegetation zones are different.

4 **a** Copy **D** and match up letters **A** to **E** with the following labels: arable fields; alpine huts; alpine pasture; coniferous woodland; deciduous woodland.
   b Draw on your diagram the routes used for transhumance in July. Explain what is meant by transhumance.

5 **C** relates to a hill farm in Britain.
   a What livestock is kept on the farm?
   b What happens to this livestock in winter?
   c What are the farmer's sources of income?
   d Which part of the farm is most productive?
   e Explain the variations in productivity for each part of the farm.

14 : The Changing Coastline

Wave Action

Coastlines are always changing through the natural processes of **erosion, transportation** and **deposition**. Ocean waves are the main factors in these changes. Waves are generated by friction between wind and the ocean surface: the stronger the wind, or the longer the wind blows from one direction, the larger the waves.

Wave size is also affected by the **fetch**, the distance of open water over which the wind travels (**A**). This means that shorelines facing a narrow stretch of water will receive smaller waves than shorelines along the margins of oceans.

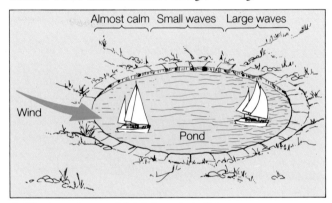

A The importance of fetch for wave size

On a gently sloping sea-bed, the waves touch bottom and break a long way from the coast. This usually results in a series of sand banks and offshore bars or ridges. However, when there is deep water close inshore, the full force of the waves is felt on the shoreline.

Large steep waves, particularly winter storm waves, are **destructive** (**B**a). They tend to crash vertically onto the beach, eroding the loose material. Smaller, short waves like those found on calm summer days are **constructive** since they push material up the beach (**B**b).

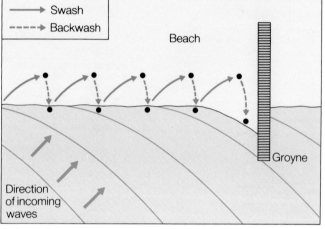

C Longshore drift

Coastal Deposition

Beaches are formed from deposits brought down by rivers, from sea floor deposits and from the erosion of cliffs.

When waves break at an angle to the beach, the swash moves up the beach, carrying sand and shingle. Any water which has not sunk into the beach is then pulled straight back down it by gravity, carrying some material with it. The result is a zig zag movement of material along the coast called **longshore drift** (**C**).

Where the coastline changes direction at a headland, bay or estuary, sand and shingle often continue to move in the direction of longshore drift. This creates long, narrow ridges called spits (**D** and **E**).

Continued deposition in sheltered bays and estuaries can result in harbours silting up. The Cinque Ports of Kent and Sussex – Rye, Winchelsea, Romney, Hythe and Sandwich – were important in the Middle Ages but they silted up and lost their trade. They now lie inland.

(a) Destructive

(b) Constructive

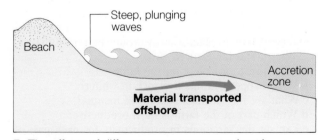

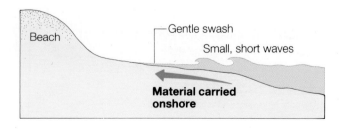

B The effects of different wave types on a beach

F Flamborough Head in North Yorkshire

Coastal Erosion

The average rate of coastal erosion is usually only about 1cm a year, but is more rapid in weak, uncemented rocks such as sands, gravels and clays. More resistant rocks such as limestone and granite are most vulnerable along lines of weakness such as **joints** and **bedding planes**.

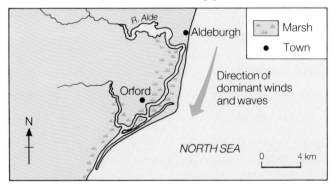

D Orford Ness in Suffolk

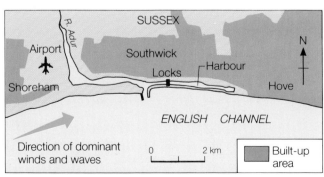

E Shoreham Spit in Sussex

Waves attack rocks in several ways:
- the pressure exerted by a storm wave can briefly reach up to 30 tonnes per square metre. Such waves can erode soft, uncemented rocks and break up rocks which contain small cracks or joints.
- air trapped by water in cracks in the rock can enlarge the cracks as it escapes with explosive force.
- pebbles and other loose material are thrown ashore, sometimes well above the normal high tide level.
- some rocks and minerals are chemically attacked by sea water and spray.

As a result, caves and arches are formed, cliff faces retreat and flat rocky **wavecut platforms** are created at the base of cliffs.

1 Study A, then answer these questions:
   a What is the meaning of the term fetch?
   b What effect does the fetch have on wave height?
   c What effect does wind duration have on wave height?
   d Look at an atlas. Which coasts of Britain have the greatest fetch?
   e Which coasts in Britain would you expect to have the smallest waves on average? Why?
2 **a** What do the terms destructive and constructive mean?
   b Explain why some waves are destructive and some are constructive.
3 Study **F**. Does it show a coast affected mainly by erosion or deposition? Explain the features shown in the photograph.

31

15 : Waves of Destruction

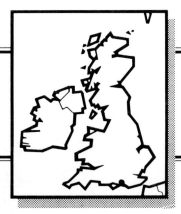

UNDER NATURAL conditions, as the sea coast retreats through erosion, the beach retreats with it. In the most vulnerable areas where weak, uncemented sands and clays face powerful storm waves, the rate of coastal retreat can be up to 6 m per year. Such erosion has always been a problem for people living in coastal areas, but it has become more significant in recent years as coastal plains and clifftops have been increasingly developed for building and tourism. Public demand for authorities to protect land and property from the sea is higher than ever before.

People try to stop or slow down coastal erosion by maintaining a beach to protect the shoreline, and by building a variety of sea defences (**A**). This is a very expensive process. Sea defences such as concrete walls, wooden groynes and breakwaters cost up to £1 million per kilometre. The processes of coastal erosion and deposition are also very complex. While sea defences in one location can stop erosion and longshore drift, this may deprive other sites of beach material. Preventing erosion in one place can increase erosion further along the coast.

The Battle of Barton On the south coast of Britain, the worst case of erosion is found at Barton in Christchurch Bay. This is partly because Barton faces the full force of the prevailing wind and dominant waves from the south-west. But it is also the result of local geology (**D**).

The upper cliff consists of **permeable** sands, silts and gravel. Rainwater easily sinks through this until it reaches an **impermeable** layer of clay. The water then collects on top of this, inside the permeable rocks, softening the clay until the land suddenly slips. The combined action of wave attack and landslip caused the cliffs to recede at an average 1 metre a year during the 1950's and early 1960's.

Not surprisingly, the residents demanded action from the local authorities to prevent their clifftop homes and guesthouses from sliding into the sea. Engineers came up with a two-part answer: protect the base of the cliffs from wave attack, and stabilise the slipping cliff face (**D**).

- Wave erosion was reduced using wooden groynes to trap beach material carried by longshore drift. Behind these were open wooden piles backed by a rock-filled trench.

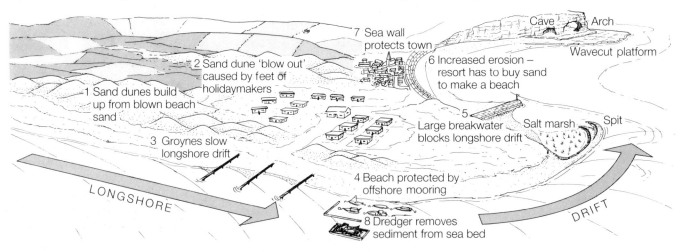

A The interaction between coastal processes and human activity

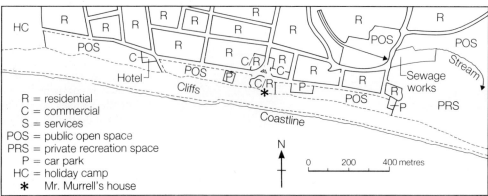

R = residential
C = commercial
S = services
POS = public open space
PRS = private recreation space
P = car park
HC = holiday camp
∗ = Mr. Murrell's house

B Barton on Sea (1976)

C Mr Jack Murrell inspects the cliff edge just outside his front door

A barrier of interlocking sheet steel piles was sunk into the clay to trap groundwater. This was then drained into the sea by a system of pipes. The steepness of the cliff face was reduced by bulldozing part of the undercliff.

The main works were completed by 1968. As public confidence rose, new building took place on the clifftop. But in February 1974, the worst storms in a century breached the wooden piles and saturated the undercliff. Repairs were under way in November 1974 when 10 days of heavy rain were followed by subsidence of the lower undercliff. The sheet piling barrier was bent forward and more than 200 metres of the drainage system was destroyed.

Despite attempts to slow the movement, another major slip occurred on 17 April, 1975. Mr. Jack Murrell awoke to find his house within a metre of the cliff edge (**C**). The house had to be abandoned and demolished.

Local residents and engineers were forced to admit that some coastal erosion at Barton is inevitable. New efforts to protect clifftop property continue with rock strongpoints in place of groynes, a sloping stone wall in place of the timber piles, and continued beach feeding by bringing in supplies of sand and gravel.

(**a**) Before the 1960s

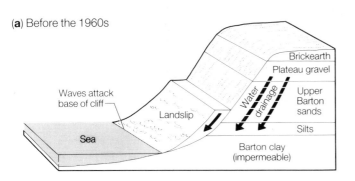

(**b**) 1960's defences

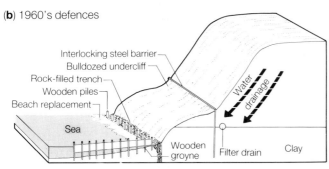

D Coastal erosion and defences at Barton

1 **a** Name two factors which make Barton vulnerable to coastal erosion.
   b Name the features shown on **B** which are most at risk from erosion.
   c Copy **B**, then shade in the area you would protect from erosion. Give reasons for your choice.
   d How long is the area you have chosen? At a cost of £1 million per kilometre, how much would your coastal defences cost altogether?

2 **a** Make a list of the measures taken to prevent coastal erosion at Barton.
   b For each of these measures, briefly explain how it was intended to solve the erosion problem.
   c Why have these measures not been successful?

3 Study **A**. List the ways in which human activity can affect the coastal environment. For each of these activities, explain how they are **a** beneficial, **b** harmful to the natural environment.

33

16 : Holding Back the Tides

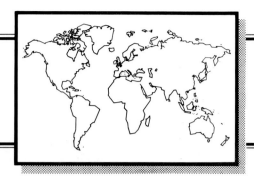

The River Thames

Mean sea level is steadily rising in south-east England by about 2 mm per year, as the crust slowly sinks. When certain storm conditions occur in the North Sea, low-lying areas are vulnerable to flooding.

Central London has been flooded many times. The most recent flood was in 1928 when 14 people drowned. An even worse disaster was narrowly avoided in 1953, when the flood waters which killed 300 people on the East Coast of England and the Thames Estuary did not quite reach the city. If a major flood did occur in London, it has been estimated that 1½ million people would be at risk, about 125 sq. km of land would be affected, and the cost of damage would be about £3,500 million.

London had to be protected from such a disaster. Instead of simply making the existing river walls and embankments higher, the Greater London Council decided on a £350 million flood barrier at Woolwich. This barrier is about 520 metres long, with six gates set between concrete piers. The barrier was completed in 1982.

A The Thames Flood Barrier ▲

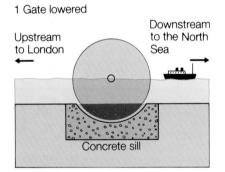

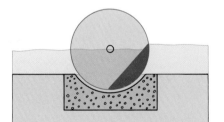

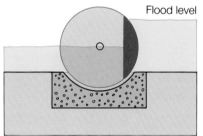

▲ **B** How the Thames Barrier operates

C The London flood risk area

Year	Height above mean sea level (m)
1791	4.21
1834	4.51
1852	4.60
1874	4.72
1875	4.82
1881	4.91
1928	5.24
1953	5.35

D Maximum high tide levels at London Bridge

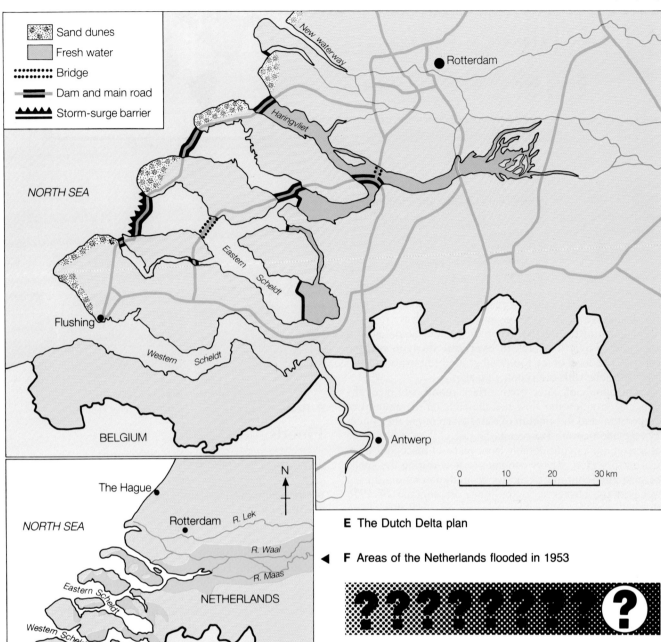

Sand dunes
Fresh water
Bridge
Dam and main road
Storm-surge barrier

NORTH SEA

New waterway

Rotterdam

Haringvliet

Eastern Scheldt

Flushing

Western Scheldt

BELGIUM

Antwerp

0   10   20   30 km

E The Dutch Delta plan

The Hague

NORTH SEA

Rotterdam   R. Lek

R. Waal

R. Maas

Eastern Scheldt

NETHERLANDS

Western Scheldt

Antwerp

BELGIUM

0   20   40 km

N

F Areas of the Netherlands flooded in 1953

The Dutch Delta Plan

The 1953 floods hit the low-lying Netherlands even harder than England: 1800 people were killed, 150,000 hectares of land were flooded, 9,000 buildings were destroyed and damage was put at £120 million. Future risks were obviously high, with half the country lying below sea level.

The Dutch answer was to block off all coastal inlets in the Rhine-Meuse delta except the Western Scheldt, and the New Waterway which links Rotterdam to the sea. This plan was later modified. The proposed dam at the mouth of the Eastern Scheldt was replaced by a storm-surge barrier, rather like the Thames barrier. This left the Eastern Scheldt as a tidal estuary with the natural environment unaffected.

? ? ? ? ? ? ?

1 **a** Which London boroughs were most at risk from a Thames flood before the barrier was built? Give a reason for your answer.
   b Which London boroughs are now most at risk from a Thames flood?
   c Suggest why the Thames barrier was located at Woolwich.
   d Copy **B**. Briefly explain how the Thames barrier works.
   e Suggest two reasons why the need for the Thames Barrier became greater.
2 **a** Why are the Netherlands more at risk from floods than southern England?
   b Why was it decided to leave open the New Waterway and Western Scheldt?
   c How long is the Eastern Scheldt storm-surge barrier?
   d Why have two lines of dams been built in the Delta Plan?
   e Compare **E** and **F**. What changes have taken place in the geography of the region as a result of the Delta Plan?

35

17 : Rivers: Friend or Foe?

THE WORLD'S RIVERS have always attracted human activity. What happens to these rivers is therefore of vital importance to billions of people.

Most of the water which feeds streams and rivers comes from rainfall or melting snow. The ground acts as a giant sponge, soaking up any water it receives. Rain falling onto the land surface usually sinks or **infiltrates** into the ground through tiny spaces called **pores**. This water may remain as **soil moisture** or move lower into the underlying rocks to become **groundwater** (A). When the ground cannot absorb any more water, it results in **overland flow** or **surface runoff**. The level of the saturated ground (the **water table**) rises and falls with the supply of water.

The supply of water from surface runoff, soil through-flow and groundwater flow also depends on the amount of evaporation and the amount of water taken out of the system by vegetation cover. As a result, the rate of flow or discharge of a river varies considerably from place to place and from season to season. Rivers continue to flow during dry spells because they continue to receive groundwater stored during wet periods. However, as the long, dry summer of 1976 showed, even the rivers of Britain can dry up if there is no rain, and if evaporation is high.

Plant cover intercepts rain and snow as it falls. This may then evaporate back into the atmosphere without reaching the ground. Plants also take up large amounts of water through their roots which is then given off through the leaves as transpiration. Trees, however, shade the ground and reduce wind speed so that evaporation rates are lower under forests.

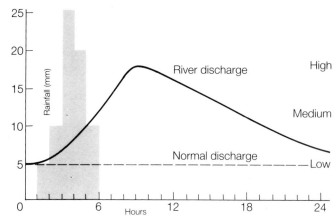

B Relationship between rainfall and river discharge

Floods

Most rivers overflow their banks at least once every two years. The flood plain close to the river is therefore of limited use to people for farming or building. Buildings near rivers are vulnerable because rivers are more powerful in times of high discharge, and more likely to erode their banks.

A particularly dangerous situation arises when rivers such as the Mississippi in the USA raise themselves above the surrounding land by building **levees**. These embankments are created as the river drops sediment on its bed and banks. As the river raises its bed above the flood plain, the only way to prevent disastrous floods is to continually build artificial levees to keep ahead of the river level.

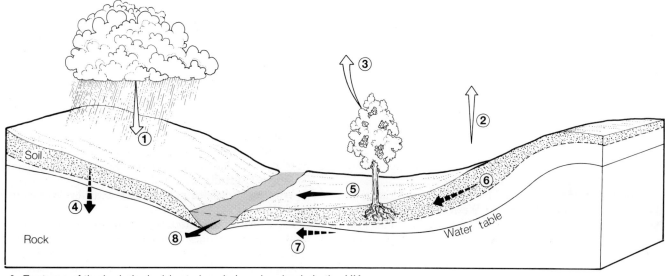

A Features of the hydrological (water) cycle in a river basin in the UK

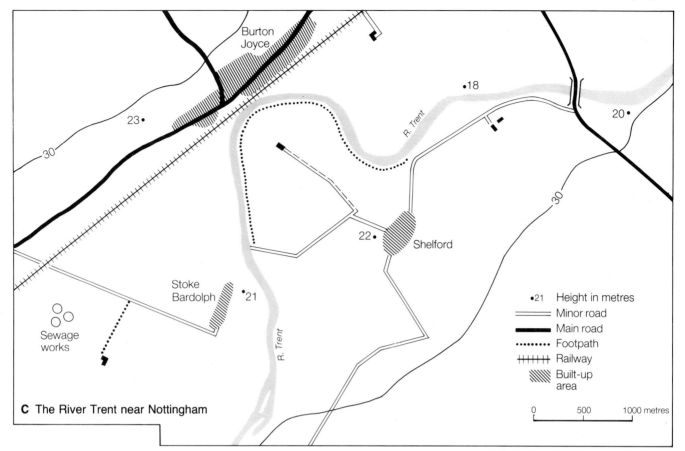

C The River Trent near Nottingham

•21	Height in metres
	Minor road
	Main road
··········	Footpath
┼┼┼┼┼	Railway
▨▨▨	Built-up area

0   500   1000 metres

Huge amounts of money are spent to prevent flood damage. Banks and walls of earth, brick or concrete are common. Weirs and dams control river levels. Land of low value beside the river is set aside for deliberate flooding during periods of high discharge so that built-up areas downstream may be protected. Large river bends or meanders are cut off and straightened to increase the river's rate of flow and so transport water more quickly to the sea.

Human activity also makes floods more likely. Destruction of vegetation means that water is not held in the soil and surface runoff increases. This, in turn, causes faster soil erosion so that rivers become clogged with sediment and flooding occurs.

Hard, **impermeable** surfaces in towns and cities allow no infiltration. Rain simply flows over the surface, down drains and into rivers. Unlike the natural system, there is hardly any soaking up of water by soil or rock, and no time

lag before the water enters the river (**D**). Nearby drains and rivers have to be able to cope with a sudden increase in the water inflow or flash flooding will occur.

1   List the types of human activity that take place on or alongside rivers.
2   Copy **A**. Then add these labels to the correct numbers in the key: soil moisture, evaporation, precipitation, runoff, groundwater flow, stream flow, infiltration, transpiration.
3   Study **B**, then answer the following questions:
    a What was the total rainfall in mm?
    b How many hours did the storm last?
    c How many hours after the storm began did the river reach maximum flow?
    d What does the area above the dashed line represent?
    e Explain why maximum discharge was much later than maximum rainfall.
    f Why did river discharge fall more slowly than it rose?
4   **a** Describe the differences between the hydrographs for an urban area and a rural area (**D**).
    b Explain why these hydrographs are so different.
5   **a** Describe ways in which people can control flooding.
    b Copy or trace **C**. On the map, mark and label any flood control measures you would introduce.
    c Describe and explain the measures you chose in **b**.

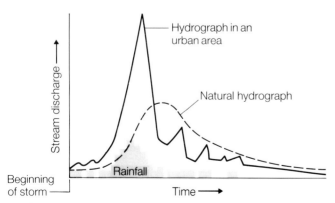

D Flood hydrographs for urban and rural areas

18 : The Flooding of York

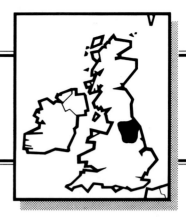

THE CITY OF YORK suffered serious flooding in 1892, 1947, 1978 and 1982. Flooding occurs when the River Ouse rises more than 4m above its normal level. The flooding of January 1982 was the result of heavy rain combined with melting snow in the Ouse catchment area. The river rapidly rose more than 5 metres above normal, flooding over 540 residential and industrial premises. Sewers overflowed, existing flood defences were damaged, and the waterworks narrowly escaped inundation.

Land in the valley of the River Foss was also affected (**F**). The commercial and industrial life of the city was brought to a standstill for three days. Many roads, including the inner ring road, were under 1 metre of water with traffic disruption over a wide area. The estimated cost of damage and disruption was £1.8 million.

A Aerial view of the city in January 1982

1 **a** Describe the relief and drainage of the Yorkshire/ Humberside area.
b Explain why the location of York makes the city vulnerable to sudden floods.
c What is the average number of years between each major flood in York?
d Why does this average figure not give a very accurate picture?
e Which areas experienced the highest snowfall 13-31 December 1981?
f Describe the pattern of rainfall 1–6 January 1982.

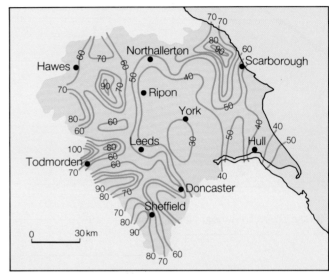

B Snowfall (water equivalent – mm) 13th–31st December 1981

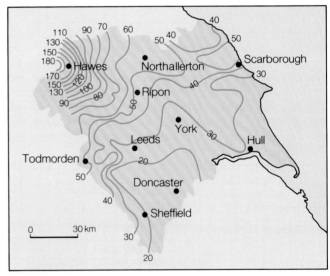

C Rainfall (mm) 1st–6th January 1982

g Why was there no flooding in York until 4 January?
h How high above normal did the river reach at its peak in 1982?
2 **a** What kind of problems resulted from the 1982 floods?
b Explain the measures being introduced to prevent further floods.
c The flood controls will cost £6.7 million. Write a report for the water authority and the city council justifying this expenditure.

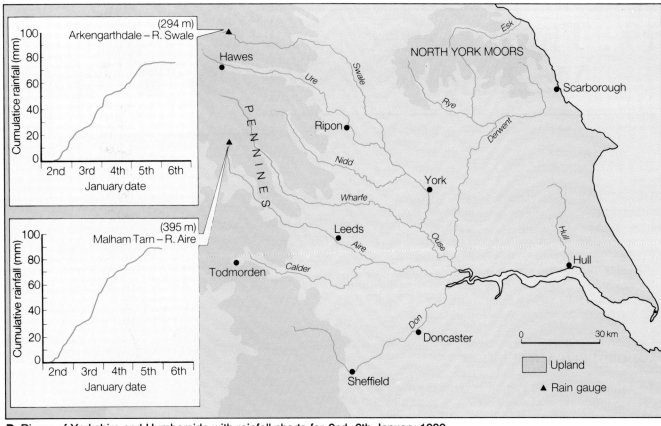

D Rivers of Yorkshire and Humberside with rainfall charts for 2nd–6th January 1982

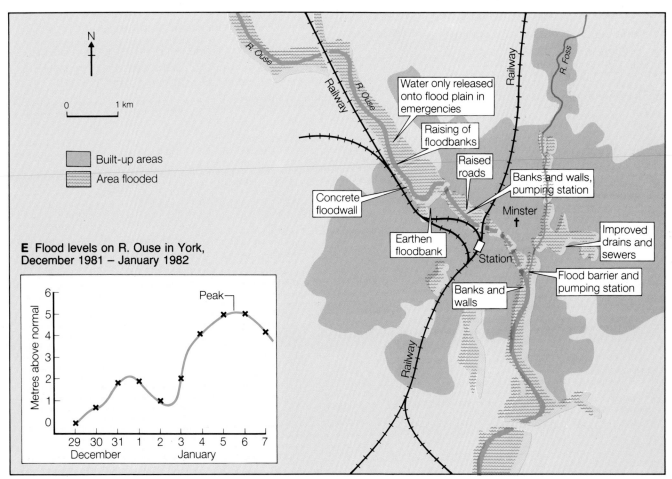

E Flood levels on R. Ouse in York,
December 1981 – January 1982

F The 1982 floods in York and new flood prevention measures

19 : The Weather Machine

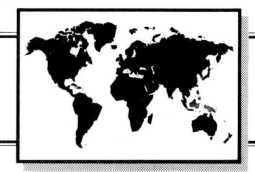

PLANET EARTH is blanketed by an atmosphere about 500 km deep, but 90% of the gases in the atmosphere occur within 10 km of the surface. This lower layer of the atmosphere, known as the **troposphere**, is the zone of weather.

Earth's weather machine is driven by heat from the sun. The atmosphere and oceans spread this heat from the warm tropics to the colder regions at higher latitudes. It is this heat which provides the energy to fuel storms.

Atmospheric Circulation

The warmest part of the Earth is between the tropics. This is because the Sun is almost directly overhead all year, so that the heat is concentrated over a small area (see **A**).

Since warm air is lighter than cold air, it tends to rise. This explains why there is a zone of rising air close to the Equator (**C**). As the air rises, it cools and releases its water vapour in the form of heavy downpours. Equatorial regions therefore tend to be hot and wet all year.

The rising air spreads out at the top of the troposphere, and moves towards higher latitudes. At about 30 degrees latitude, the upper air begins to sink back to the surface, creating high pressure zones or **anticyclones**. This sinking air prevents the formation of rain clouds, so there is a belt of hot deserts.

Air spreads out from these **horse latitude highs** to create the trade winds and the westerlies which were so useful in the days of sailing ships. Where the warm westerlies meet cold air from the polar regions, a continual battle for supremacy takes place. The wave-shaped war zone

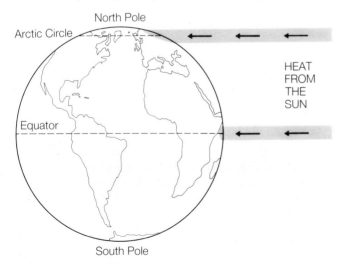

A The influence of latitude on solar heating

North Pole
Arctic Circle
Equator
South Pole

HEAT FROM THE SUN

B Earth's weather seen from space

is called the **polar front**. It is the source of storms called **depressions** which bring rain and high winds to mid-latitude countries such as Britain, Japan, New Zealand and Chile.

The Water Cycle

Life on Earth depends on a regular and adequate supply of water. This water moves through a cycle (**D**). Heat from the sun causes water from the surface of land or sea to **evaporate**, so that it changes into an invisible gas called **water vapour**. If the water vapour in the atmosphere cools below its **dew point temperature**, it **condenses** or changes back into liquid water. These water droplets form clouds and **precipitation**, usually rain. This returns to the surface and feeds back into the cycle.

The Changing Climate

In an ideal world, we would be able to predict what climatic conditions will be like from records of the past. However, this is not the case. Weather conditions vary greatly from day to day and from year to year. This unreliability makes life very difficult for people who work outdoors and have to protect themselves against storms, frost, drought, and floods.

Although we now use satellites and powerful computers, the workings of the weather machine are not clearly understood. Forecasting is very unreliable even over a few

Changing the Atmosphere 96–97 · Drought in the Sahel 52–53 · The Urban Climate 98–99
Tropical Storms 42–43 · Depressions 48–49 · Cyclones in Bangladesh 44–45
Thunderstorms and Tornadoes 46–47 · The Spreading Deserts 50–51

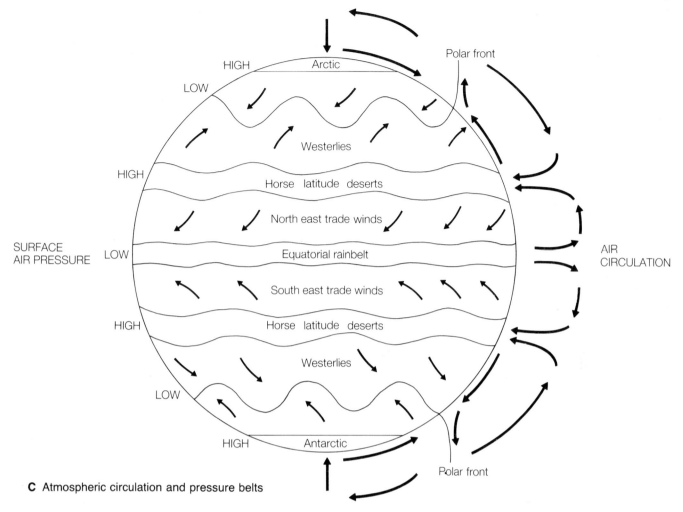

C Atmospheric circulation and pressure belts

days. Long term changes in the weather can have dramatic effects on the local economy, as happened recently in the Sahel region of Africa and in the Dust Bowl of the United States in the 1930's. We have no way of controlling weather activity, but we can alter the atmosphere by careless human activities such as the destruction of forests and burning of fossil fuels. Both of these activities change the balance established over millions of years.

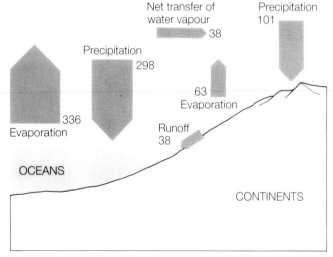

D The water cycle

1 Write a sentence explaining the meaning of each of these terms:
   a troposphere **b** evaporation **c** condensation **d** precipitation
2 Complete these sentences using the correct word:
   a Air cools when it . . . . . .
   b When rising air cools, it results in the formation of . . . . . . and rain.
   c The equatorial region is hot all year because the Sun is always . . . . in the sky.
   d The equatorial region is wet all year because there is a belt of . . . . rising air.
   e There are deserts at 30 degrees latitude because there is a zone of . . . . pressure where air is sinking.

3 Study **D**, then answer these questions:
   a Where does most evaporation take place?
   b Where does most precipitation take place?
   c How does water return to the ocean from the continents?
4 Study the weather photograph. With the help of an atlas, name the regions affected by **a** the equatorial rain belt, **b** the horse latitude high pressure belt, and **c** the polar front.

41

20 : Tropical Storms

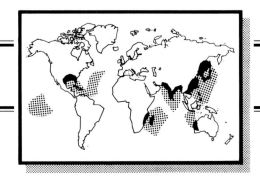

EVERY YEAR tropical and sub-tropical coastal regions and islands are lashed by the most powerful storms on Earth. They are most commonly known as hurricanes, although in the Pacific and Asia they are called cyclones or typhoons. Every year hundreds, perhaps thousands, of people die and millions of pounds worth of damage is caused by these storms.

What Is A Hurricane? Hurricanes are born over very warm oceans. They can occur at any time of year, although they are most frequent from May to December. They begin as areas of heavy showers where warm, moist air rises and cools to form rain clouds thousands of metres high. As this air rises, an area of low air pressure develops. Due to Earth's rotation, the clouds begin to spin around the low pressure centre. They pick up speed and suck up huge amounts of moisture. The centre of the storm – called the eye – is an area of descending air, marked by clear skies (**C**).

Hurricanes in June, July, October and November generally last only about a week, but the monsters of mid-season may grow into storms over 800 km across and batter tropical waters for two weeks or more. When hurricanes drift over land and/or away from the Equator, they begin to die. This is because they need a warm ocean power source to feed them warm, humid air.

A A hurricane as seen from space

Frequency of tropical storms
(per decade)

→ 10–30

➤ 30–60

▨ Sea temperatures over 27°C in warmest month

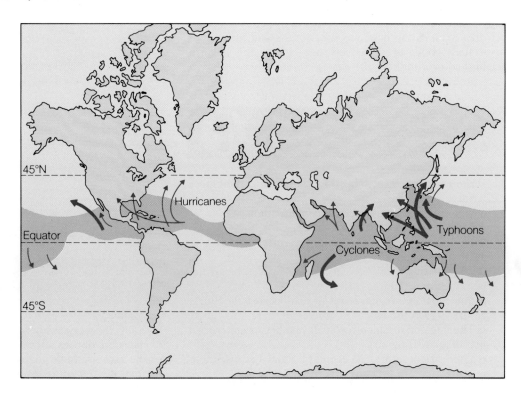

B Tropical storm tracks

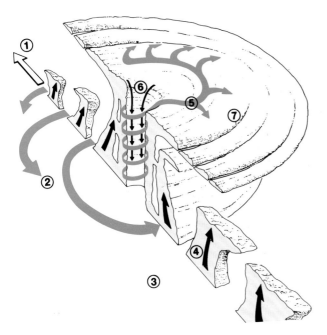

C Cross-section through a hurricane

D Storm damage from a cyclone

The Distribution Of Hurricanes Hurricanes develop over the sun-warmed tropical waters of the Atlantic, Pacific and Indian Oceans. They are generally carried along by the trade winds, then curve away from the Equator around the horse latitude high pressure areas (see unit 19). Countries along these routes suffer heavily, particularly in the Caribbean and south east Asia (**B**).

The Effects Hurricanes destroy lives and property in three main ways:

- Wind speeds of more than 200 km/h uproot trees, flatten crops and houses, turn over cars and batter shipping.
- Very low air pressure combined with high winds can raise the ocean surface into a giant bulge called a storm surge. When this hits land it flattens coastal settlements and floods wide areas.
- Very heavy rainfall adds to flooding and crop damage.

Prediction and Prevention Modern radar and weather satellites make detecting and tracking hurricanes much easier than in the past. However, exact predictions are difficult to make because hurricanes often suddenly change course. When hurricanes threaten the United States, special aircraft fly into the storms to relay accurate information to the US National Hurricane Centre.

Warnings are then sent out to all areas under threat so that houses can be boarded up, boats moored in sheltered harbours and people evacuated. In spite of these precautions, since 1900 hurricanes have caused more than 12 billion (12,000,000,000) dollars worth of damage and killed more than 13,000 people in the United States. In poorer countries the death toll is often much higher (see unit 21).

Attempts have been made by the United States to prevent the build-up of hurricanes. Between 1961 and 1971, four hurricanes were 'seeded' by aircraft carrying silver iodide crystals. Results were promising. The supply of warm, moist air to the eye was reduced, causing the eye to expand and the wind speed to drop by up to 30%. However, this work is still in the experimental stage.

1 Study **B**, then answer these questions:
   a Hurricanes are found in the_____ Ocean.
   Typhoons are found in the_____ Ocean.
   Cyclones are found in the_____ Ocean.
   b Which region suffers most often from tropical storms?
   c Which tropical ocean has no tropical storms? Why?
   d What is the highest latitude that tropical storms normally reach?

2 **a** Draw a large copy of **C**, then add a key to the numbers using the labels given below:

Warm ocean	Spiral rainband
Eye	High altitude spreading air
Path of storm	Strong anticlockwise wind
Dense cloud layer	

   b Why are tropical storms born over warm oceans?
   c Why do tropical storms die (i) over land, (ii) at high latitudes?

3 Below is some advice given to people during storm warnings. Give reasons for each item:

Advice	Reason
Turn on your radio	
Store 3 days' water and food	
Store paraffin lamps or candles	
Reinforce windows, roofs and doors	
Keep first aid kit handy	
Have clothes and essentials packed	
Remain indoors	
Keep calm	

4 Explain why less-developed countries are likely to suffer more property damage and loss of life from hurricanes than developed countries.

43

21 : Cyclones in Bangladesh

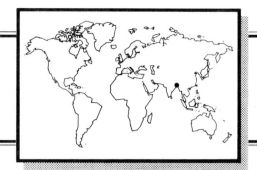

BANGLADESH is one of the world's poorest countries. Nearly all of its population live and work in the countryside. They are **subsistence** farmers who rely on intensive rice farming for their livelihood, although fishing is an important occupation along the coast.

Most of the country is flat and low-lying since it is located on the huge delta where the rivers Ganges and Brahmaputra join before entering the sea. Shifting islands of silt are created and destroyed every year by the river floodwaters. Around 5 million people cultivate the fertile silt, producing high yields of rice which prevent serious food shortages. However, rapidly increasing population puts pressure on farmers so that they colonise the less fertile and more dangerous flood plains near the coast.

The Setting for Disaster

The Bay of Bengal is one of the most dangerous places in the world for tropical cyclones. Although there are on average only six cyclones per year in the Bay of Bengal, the people of Bangladesh are vulnerable to major disasters. The following factors each contribute to these disasters:

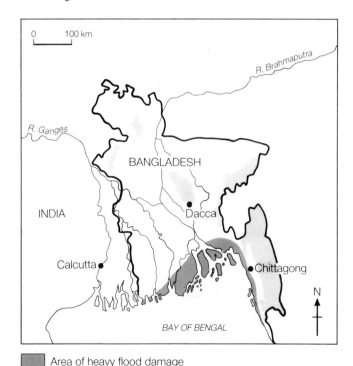

A Cyclone damage in Bangladesh, 1985

Area of heavy flood damage

Upland above normal flood level

B Ganges Delta seen from space

- Most of the country is low-lying. 'Tidal waves' can flood huge areas, including entire islands.
- There are many rivers and canals which spread flood water across a wide area.
- Floodwaters come downriver from rain in India and Nepal as well as upriver from tidal surges.
- The shape of the coast funnels water so that it piles up into storm surges more than eight metres high.
- The high population density means that many people are affected in a small area which makes evacuation difficult.
- Buildings cannot withstand severe storms or flood. Most houses are made from local materials such as bamboo and are built on wooden stilts to avoid normal floodwater.
- There are no coastal defences, partly due to the poverty of the country, and partly due to the great difficulty in constructing them.
- The lack of advance warning systems and poor communications gives little opportunity to predict and prevent a disaster.

A Tragic History

Cyclones appear with frightening regularity over Bangladesh. During the period 1960–81, the country was struck by 37 cyclones, far more than any other country in the world. The official death toll for the period was 386,200 people. However, this is almost certainly an underestimate.

Relief organisations estimate that between 500,000 and 1 million people died as a result of a single storm which devastated the country in November 1970. The numbers of dead at this time were swollen by vast numbers of migrant workers who had arrived to help with the harvest after the summer monsoon. The death toll also includes the later deaths from disease and famine.

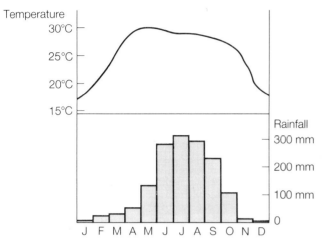

C Climate graph for Dacca (Bangladesh)

	Bangladesh	United Kingdom
Population density /km^2	602	229
Annual population growth rate (%)	3.0	0.1
Protein intake in grammes per person per day	41	91
Average annual income (US dollars)	130	7,920
% working in agriculture	74	2
% access to safe water	53	100
% change in food production since 1971	−6	+18

E Comparison between UK and Bangladesh

Cyclone death toll 'may reach 40,000'

By MUFAZZAL HUSAIN in Dacca

Thousands of bodies are floating in the Bay of Bengal in the aftermath of the cyclone and 45ft tidal wave which hit the coast region of Bangladesh last Friday.

Three thousand bodies have been recovered so far, but unofficial estimates put the death toll at up to 40,000.

An official source in the district of Noakhali said 6,000 people were washed away into the Bay of Bengal.

Communications with the coastal areas and islands of the region are not yet fully restored but a spokesman at the disaster central headquarters in Dacca said at least 12,000 people were missing from seven islands which took the brunt of the tidal wave.

'Worst Tragedy'

President Ershad, who has cancelled a visit to China due to start today, described the wave as the "worst tragedy in Bangladesh's history".

About 250,000 people have lost their homes and President Ershad has mobilised the three armed services on a war footing to provide relief services.

Helicopters are dropping food and drinking water to survivors and navy ships are ploughing through rain and heavy seas to reach cut-off islands.

One report said hundreds of survivors on bamboo rafts and floating rooftops were being stalked by sharks and crocodiles as they awaited rescue.

A survivor said he spent 48 hours clinging to his wooden bed before a ship picked him up about 20 miles out to sea.

The Bangladesh Navy said a search ship, the Darshak, had picked up 100 bodies and rescued about 1,000 people from the sea near the island of Sandwip.

A 15-year-old girl described how she lost her parents, two brothers and a sister.

"We were all sleeping in the same hut, but when the cyclone came all the others vanished and I was jammed against a fallen tree," she said.

Rescue officials were concerned about the fate of 2,000 people living on the furthermost island of Uri Char, about 25 miles off Chittagong.

Navy and army teams scouring the island and surrounding seas have so far found no sign of life.

The full extent of the disaster is unlikely to be known until the ships reached several low-lying mud islands mainly populated by fishermen.

But the plight of the survivors is known to be desperate as the sea has washed away their food supplies, polluted their drinking water and ruined crops.

D The 1985 cyclone disaster in Bangladesh

1. Explain the meaning of the following terms:
   a delta **b** silt **c** migrant **d** population density
2. **a** Why are houses in Bangladesh often built on stilts?
   b Study **C**. At which time of year are the rivers most likely to flood?
   c Why do the people of Bangladesh normally welcome the floods?
   d Study **A**. What was the area of land flooded by the 1985 tidal wave?
   e Why are the Bangladesh figures for deaths due to cyclones so unreliable?
3. Complete **F** by naming the main factors which influence cyclone disasters.
4. Read the newspaper article from 26 May 1985 (**D**). Explain what problems resulted from the cyclone.
5. **a** Study **E**. Which of those statistics help to explain why the people of Bangladesh continue to farm areas which are vulnerable to tidal waves?
   b Explain your choice.
6. Outline some of the policies you would put forward to solve the cyclone problem in Bangladesh: **a** in the short term, **b** in the long term.

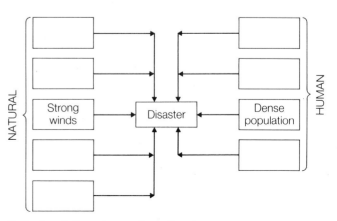

F Factors influencing cyclone disasters

22 : Thunderstorms and Tornadoes

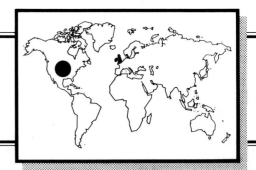

MAJOR STORMS are not restricted to the tropics. Every year, millions of pounds' worth of damage is caused by thunderstorms and tornadoes.

Thunderstorms   Thunderstorms can cause great damage through strong winds, heavy rain, hail and lightning. At any moment there are about 500 thunderstorms across the world, with perhaps 100 lightning strikes every second.

The bolts of electrical energy which we call lightning are generated in towering **cumulonimbus** clouds which reach to the top of the troposphere, an altitude of about 12 km. These clouds are the result of **convection currents** in the air (**A**). Air is warmed by the ground, then expands and bubbles upwards like a hot air balloon. If the air is warmed sufficiently, it can rapidly rise above the level at which clouds form. At the **tropopause** (the upper boundary of the troposphere) the rising air spreads out, forming a flat, anvil-shaped cloud (**B**).

The tops of these clouds are so high and so cold that they are made of ice crystals and water droplets supercooled below normal freezing point. Air currents inside the cloud sweep the crystals up and down. New layers freeze around the crystals until they fall to earth as hail.

Rapid motion of ice and water droplets in the cloud causes them to become electrically charged. When a negatively charged cloud passes over a positively charged ground surface, a bolt of lightning passes between them carrying millions of volts of static electricity.

Tornadoes   These funnel-shaped storms develop from thunderclouds when warm, moist air is trapped beneath

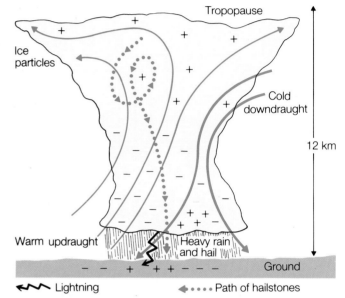

B Features of a thunderstorm

cold, dry air. The two air masses do not mix. Instead, the updraught caused by the warm, rising air is strengthened as the cold air spirals around it. As the air spins faster and the turning circle becomes smaller, a funnel of cloud descends towards the ground (**C**).

The region most vulnerable to tornadoes is the United States, where they are known as 'twisters'. Every year there are around 1000 tornadoes in the USA, mostly in summer.

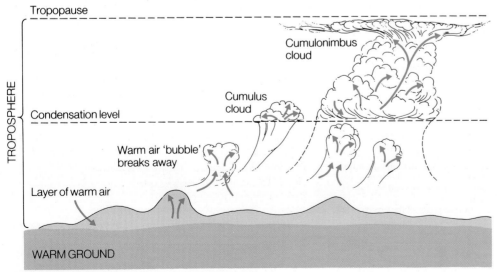

A The formation of thunderclouds through convection

C A tornado

Year	UK	USA
1970	13	649
1971	41	890
1972	20	743
1973	10	1112
1974	59	944
1975	42	920
1976	14	835
1977	9	850
1978	25	788
1979	23	847
Total	256	8578

◀ **D** Annual frequency of tornadoes in UK and USA 1970–79

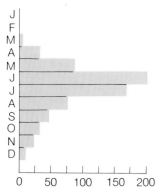

E Histogram of monthly frequencies of tornadoes in Iowa (1916–61)

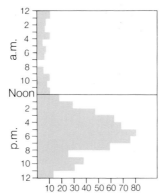

F Histogram of hourly frequency of tornadoes in Iowa (1916–61)

Weather hazard	Average annual deaths	Average annual property damage
Tornado	125	$75 million
Lightning	150	$100 million
Hail	–	$284 million
Hurricane	75	$500 million

G Damage in the USA due to severe weather

They form in the interior plains where warm, moist air from the Gulf of Mexico meets cold, dry air from Canada.

With wind speeds of 350 km/hr around the core of a tornado, people, livestock and objects weighing many tonnes can be picked up and carried considerable distances. The very low air pressure inside the funnel can cause buildings to explode if doors and windows are closed. There are even cases of bark being torn from trees, feathers from chickens, wool from sheep and clothes from people. Fortunately, tornadoes rarely last more than an hour or travel further than about 40 km. The trail of damage is very narrow, usually between 250 metres and 1 km wide.

Prediction and Prevention   Attempts have been made to stop the growth of thunderclouds by seeding them with crystals of carbon dioxide or silver iodide (see unit 20). The process may one day reduce damage from hail and rain, but this is still a long way off.

There is no known way of preventing or modifying tornadoes. Since 1973, the United States Tornado Watch has cut death rates by allowing inhabitants time to reach special shelters. Warnings can be given when conditions favour the formation of tornadoes, although their paths are very unpredictable. They can also be recognised on radar screens from the hook-shaped area of rainfall.

Tornado toll reaches 86

From our own correspondent

The death toll in the chain of tornadoes which swept through the north-eastern United States and Ontario on Friday night rose yesterday to 86, with hundreds more injured and thousands homeless.

In the state of Pennsylvania, at least 61 of the victims died and a state of emergency was declared. The tornadoes almost destroyed small towns like Atlantic, Albion, and Wheatland, together with Niles, in neighbouring Ohio, each in a matter of seconds. In one county alone damage costs were estimated at $14 million.

This is the tornado season, but what was unusual about this particularly violent collision of warm and cold air systems was that it reached unusually far north into Canada, unleashing some of its energy on the town of Barrie, 50 miles north of Toronto. At least 12 people, including several children, died there.

Upstate New York was also hit, but no one was reported killed. American officials said it was the country's worst outbreak of tornadoes since April, 1974, when 315 people died.

Routine storm warnings were issued late on Friday afternoon, but inevitably people were taken by surprise. Some described the 40-second mayhem as sounding "like a freight train" or "a jet engine".

Trees were carried half-a-mile through the air and houses destroyed or lifted off their foundations in a swathe up to 200 feet wide along a 300-mile path.

H Effects of tornadoes in N America

1   Make a list of the similarities and differences between hurricanes and tornadoes.
2   Using the statistics in **D**, draw histograms to show the annual frequency of tornadoes in the UK and USA.
3   Study **E** and **F**.
   a In which month are tornadoes most frequent in Iowa?
   b At what time of day do most tornadoes appear in Iowa?
   c Try to explain the frequencies shown in these histograms.
4   Read the newspaper article (**H**).
   a When is the tornado season?
   b Why were these tornadoes unusual?
   c What does the article tell you about the behaviour of tornadoes?
   d Look at the statistics in **G**. Describe what the table tells you. Explain why the death rates and property losses do not seem to be related.

23 : Depressions

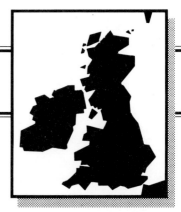

WE LIVE ON Earth's surface at the bottom of its atmosphere. Although we do not usually notice it, this atmosphere presses down on everything. The average air pressure at sea level is about 1000 mb (millibars). It can be measured by instruments called **barometers** which tell us when the air pressure is low or high. Areas of low pressure in mid-latitudes are called depressions and are associated with storms.

These storms are usually born where warm, moist air in the westerly wind belt meets colder air at the polar front. Above the polar front is a narrow, snake-like belt of strong westerly winds called the **jet stream**. When the jet stream bends towards the poles, it draws the warm air up over the colder polar air. This rising air causes the air pressure at the surface to fall. The wind speed begins to increase as a spiral air circulation (anticlockwise in the northern hemisphere) is set up.

As the depression moves eastward and grows, a wedge of warm air becomes surrounded by colder air (**A**). Two fronts mark the boundary between the air masses. Where the warm air pushes gently over the colder air, a **warm front** forms. Where the colder air pushes beneath the warm air, a **cold front** forms. In both cases, the fronts are marked by condensation, thick cloud and heavy rain (**B**). Eventually, after about a week, the cold front catches up with the warm front, and lifts the warm wedge of air off the ground completely. This is called an **occluded front** and the result is less cloud and rain.

Depressions follow the zigzag path of the jet stream, but in a typical year many of them track across Britain and western Europe before their pressure rises and the fronts disappear. This is why Britain has such a changeable climate and such a high average annual rainfall, especially in the west where depressions and fronts are more common and more active.

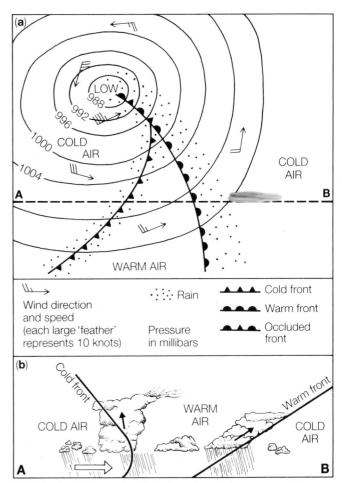

B A typical depression (a) plan view (b) cross section A–B

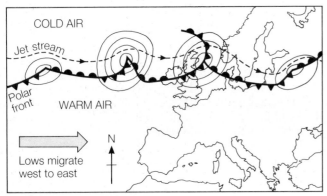

A A family of depressions, or the life cycle of one depression

??????? ?

1 Study **F** and **G**.
 a Which parts of Britain have the most wet days per year?
 b Suggest why this is the case.
 c Draw a climate graph for Falmouth.
 d In which months are depressions most likely over Falmouth?
2 Study **E**, then answer these questions:
 a Name the weather systems at **X** and **Y**.
 b Imagine you were taking weather readings on the ships

at **S** and **T**. Write a brief summary of the results for the ships' logs.

c Explain why the two sets of readings are different.

d Name at least three sources of information used by weather forecasters.

e Prepare a weather forecast for the farmers in area **Z**, explaining the changes in weather they can expect in the next 2 to 3 days.

3 Read the newspaper article for 20 November 1986 (**C**). On an outline map of southern England and Wales, label the places mentioned and the effects of the depression. Use an atlas to find the places. With the help of **A** and **B**, add a dashed line to show the route you think the depression followed.

Rain and wind bring chaos

By David Sapsted

Floods brought varying degrees of chaos to Britain yesterday.

Nobody was hurt in the autumn onslaught of torrential rain that left some Welsh families trapped after six feet of water invaded the ground floors of their homes.

Wales took the brunt of the windswept deluge: at Ystalyfera West Glamorgan, 60 houses were cut off by flood water, the A5049 to Mountain Ash was closed and extensive flooding was reported in the Builth area.

Winds gusting up to storm force 10 disrupted Channel ferry services. Several seafronts on the south coast were closed in the face of the battering.

At Fittleton, near Salisbury, more than 700 homes were left without power after a transformer was knocked out by the gale, while a tree blown across power lines near

Thruxton motor racing circuit was blamed for another 200 homes in Andover being blacked out.

Rivers overflowed in Sussex, flooding farmland and heavy seas at Hastings smashed shelters on the promenade. Police closed the A2 leading up from the docks at Dover and other seafront roads were closed at Southsea, Gosport and Southampton.

At Hurn Airport near Bournemouth high winds flipped a four-seater light aircraft onto its back, causing £6,000 damage and in the West Country an inch and a half of rain and gales brought down trees and power cables and caused flooding in Tiverton, St Austell, Bodmin, Camborne and Hayle.

The weather was also blamed for an accident near junction 10 on the southbound carriageway of the M1 that produced an eight-mile tailback.

High winds also resulted in a 40 mph speed limit being imposed on the M2 across the Medway Bridge in Kent.

British Rail blamed the weather for the disruption of some southeast commuter services yesterday morning.

C Effects of a depression

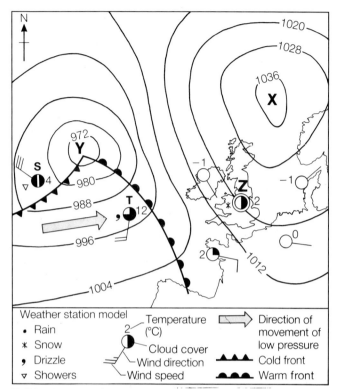

E Weather map for 15th January 1985 at midday

Weather station model
- Rain
- Snow
- Drizzle
- Showers

Temperature (°C)
Cloud cover
Wind direction
Wind speed

Direction of movement of low pressure
Cold front
Warm front

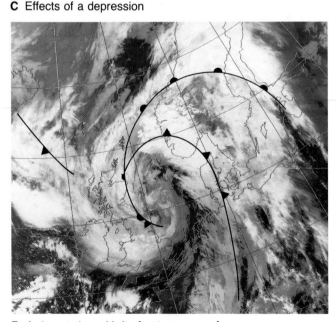

D A depression with its fronts as seen from space

F Average number of rain days per year in Britain

Over 200
175–200
Under 175

Falmouth

Falmouth	J	F	M	A	M	J	J	A	S	O	N	D
Rainfall (mm)	132	95	81	67	66	50	71	77	78	117	132	134
Temperature (°C)	4.9	4.8	5.1	6.3	8.6	11.3	13.2	12	9.4	6.6	5.1	

G Mean temperature and rainfall figures for Falmouth

24 : The Spreading Deserts

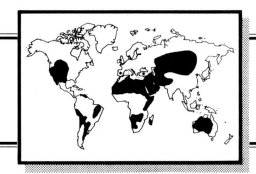

DESERTS AND SEMI-DESERTS cover about one third of the world's land surface (A). They have a very low annual rainfall, often below 250 mm, and high evaporation rates. Any rain which does fall soon sinks into the parched ground or evaporates and is of little use to farmers. Some deserts are bare sand, stones or rock, although scrub is common in deserts of Australia, Namibia and North America. Nomadic groups such as the aborigines of Australia only survived until recently by moving around in search of water and food.

Water is available alongside large, permanent rivers such as the Nile or Niger, or around an oasis, where underground water appears at the surface through springs or wells. In such places, farmers can raise crops by irrigating the land and market towns develop.

Life in the desert is always hard. Rainfall is scarce and unreliable – sometimes there is no rain for several years. Communications are often poor with only a few dirt roads. In the sandy deserts, sandstorms are a common event, and shifting sand dunes may bury fields and towns. People such as the nomadic Bedouin of the Sahara have adapted to desert life over thousands of years by moving around with their herds of camels, sheep and goats, but the deserts are now beginning to spread as new pressures destroy the delicate balance. This process is called **desertification**.

The crisis is often triggered by a change in climate and by increasing pressure on the land as new settlers and their

B Nomads on the edge of the Sahara

livestock move into the desert fringes. When numbers of people and animals rise during times of relative prosperity, the land is overgrazed, ploughed up, or stripped of trees for firewood and charcoal. People must then look further afield for new pastures or sources of fuel. The only alternative to firewood is to burn the dung which would otherwise fertilise the land.

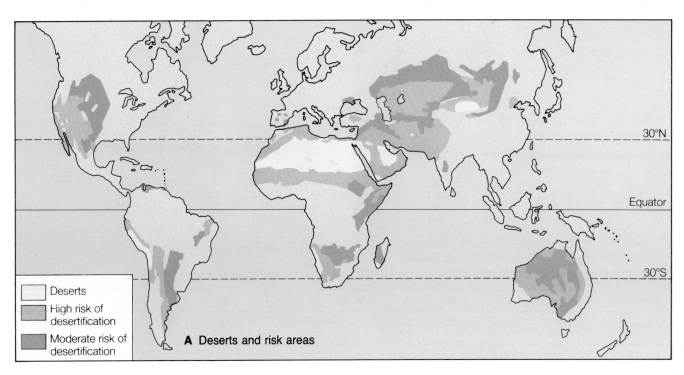

Deserts

High risk of desertification

Moderate risk of desertification

A Deserts and risk areas

30°N

Equator

30°S

50

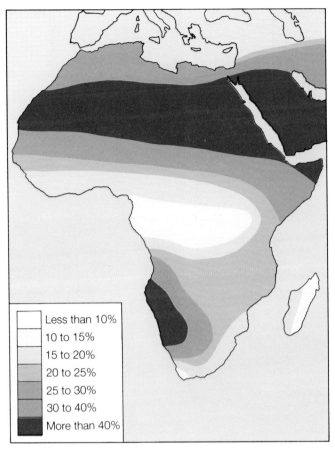

C Percentage variation in rainfall between 'high' years and 'low' years in Africa

Large numbers of animals compress the soil into a hard, solid surface which does not easily absorb rain. Traditional grazing lands may be taken over by farmers growing cash crops such as peanuts. The thin soil is exposed to erosion by wind and short, torrential rainstorms. Rills and gullies are cut by running water, and the water table drops as less water sinks into the ground, making it even more difficult for crops to grow.

When an extended period of drought arrives, the crops fail, the pasture withers and the people and animals are forced to move away or starve. This may cause conflict with other groups. The process starts all over again in the newly settled area.

There are ways of preventing the spread of deserts, but many desert countries are poor and rely on foreign aid and advice. One answer is to spend money on long-term projects such as educating the local people and reclaiming the desert. Another answer is to provide the people with better tools and seeds, and to support them in times of need.

The most obvious method of stopping desertification is to replant trees and shrubs which can prevent soil erosion, hold the water in the soil, and provide new sources of firewood. Soil erosion can also be halted by construction of small dams which hold back runoff and eroded soil. Water from these small ponds can then be used to irrigate crops. Dry farming methods also help to protect the soil (see unit 30). An extreme solution in oil-rich countries like Iran is to stabilise shifting sand by spraying it with oil before planting drought-resistant trees. None of this will have any effect, however, if the land remains overpopulated and overgrazed.

1　a On an outline map of the world, mark and name the main deserts and semi-deserts. Use an atlas to help you.
b Which continent has the largest area of desert?
c There are two belts of deserts. Give the latitudes between which these belts lie.
d Explain why the deserts lie in these belts (refer to unit 19 if you need help).
e Study **C**. What is the percentage variation in average annual rainfall in the Sahara Desert of North Africa?
f Why does this rainfall variation cause problems for the local population?

2　a Why are deserts often sparsely populated?
b How have people adapted to the deserts over many centuries?
c What does the word desertification mean?
d Which parts of the world are most at risk from desertification?

3　a Copy and complete **D**, using the labels provided.
b Explain how desertification could be slowed down or prevented.
c Imagine you are a conservationist trying to prevent desertification. Write down the arguments you would use to local people who made these statements to you:
"I need to cut down trees – they are my only source of fuel."
"I will not reduce my animal herds – they are my only source of food and wealth."
"My animals need food. I can't help it if they eat all the vegetation and trample the ground."
"I can't stay on my land if the drought kills my crops and animals."

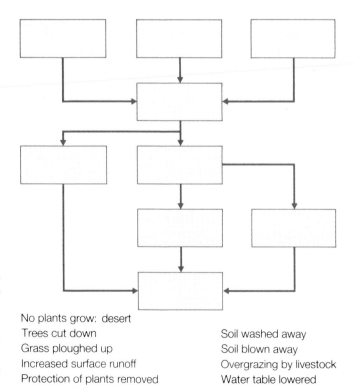

No plants grow: desert
Trees cut down
Grass ploughed up
Increased surface runoff
Protection of plants removed

Soil washed away
Soil blown away
Overgrazing by livestock
Water table lowered

D　Desertification as a result of human activity

25 : Drought in the Sahel

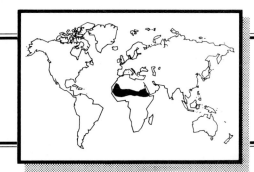

LYING JUST TO THE SOUTH of the Sahara Desert is a semi-arid zone which separates the desert from the savanna grasslands (A). This region, known as the Sahel, has traditionally been home to subsistence farmers and nomadic herders such as the Fulani. Under the bush fallowing system, land was used, then rested or left fallow so that it could recover its fertility.

From the 1940's to the late 1960's, the short summer rainfall was fairly reliable, and was often well above the annual average of 400 mm. This encouraged nomadic herders to move their cattle, sheep and goats further north into the Sahara. The former grazing lands were ploughed up. Food crops such as maize or millet were often replaced by cash crops such as groundnuts. Land was cleared for cultivation and the trees were used for fuel and for making charcoal. When the rapidly growing population demanded more food, the normal fallow period was omitted so that more crops could be grown. Then came the drought.

C A village of the Sahel surrounded by bare land

Famine

No-one was prepared for the sudden decline in rainfall which began in 1968 (E). By 1973, there was a full-scale emergency over the entire Sahel. As the pasture died and water holes dried up, herders turned south once more to their traditional grazing lands. But these were now fenced off for crops and there was little fallow land available. When the pasture ran out, the animals began to die from hunger and thirst. No-one wanted to buy cattle, so the herders were forced to kill and eat their only source of income.

Crop farmers were no better off, especially if they grew cash crops like cotton which could not be eaten. The crops withered and died in the rock-hard sunbaked ground. The soil began to blow away. Any rain that did fall simply eroded the bare, unprotected soil. Deprived of food and income, the farmers began to eat the seeds intended for the next season. After that, there was only starvation. Millions died.

The situation was made worse by civil wars in Chad, Ethiopia and Somalia. Millions flocked to refugee camps in search of food, putting tremendous pressure on governments and relief agencies. The camps were often at the end of barely passable dirt roads. There was a continual threat of epidemics due to overcrowding and poor sanitation.

The Response Large sums of money were spent by foreign governments, the United Nations, and many other relief organisations on emergency food rations and long term prevention measures. Ordinary people were encouraged to help through sponsored events organised by Band Aid and Live Aid.

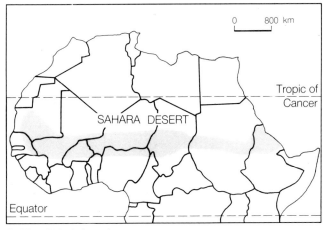

A The Sahel drought zone

Country	Pop	Annual Natural increase	Life expectancy	GDP per person
Mauritania	1.6m	2.6%	46yrs	$480
Mali	7.2m	2.5%	45yrs	$160
Burkino Faso	6.5m	2.0%	44yrs	$180
Niger	6.1m	3.2%	45yrs	$240
Chad	4.8m	2.4%	43yrs	$130
Sudan	21m	2.8%	48yrs	$400
Ethiopia	41m	2.6%	43yrs	$120

GDP = Gross Domestic Product (value of all goods and services produced in the country)

B The countries of the Sahel dought zone

52

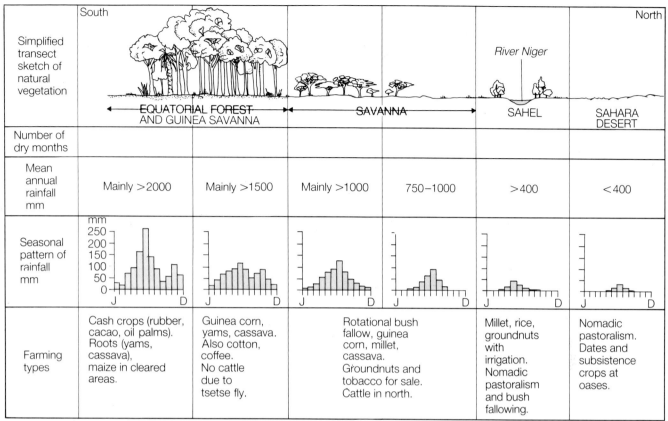

	South				River Niger	North
Simplified transect sketch of natural vegetation	EQUATORIAL FOREST AND GUINEA SAVANNA		SAVANNA		SAHEL	SAHARA DESERT
Number of dry months						
Mean annual rainfall mm	Mainly >2000	Mainly >1500	Mainly >1000	750–1000	>400	<400
Seasonal pattern of rainfall mm						
Farming types	Cash crops (rubber, cacao, oil palms). Roots (yams, cassava), maize in cleared areas.	Guinea corn, yams, cassava. Also cotton, coffee. No cattle due to tsetse fly.	Rotational bush fallow, guinea corn, millet, cassava. Groundnuts and tobacco for sale. Cattle in north.		Millet, rice, groundnuts with irrigation. Nomadic pastoralism and bush fallowing.	Nomadic pastoralism. Dates and subsistence crops at oases.

D Transect south-north across West Africa

Some extreme measures were taken. In Ethiopia, thousands of people were forcibly resettled in more fertile lands further south. More typical were the local projects to supply water for crops, animals and people by sinking wells and building small dams and canals. Tree planting began, to replace the lost vegetation and to prevent soil erosion. New seeds were given to refugees so that they could return home and start again. Local people were taught how to look after the land by levelling fields, making hillside terraces and building stone walls to retain rainfall. Draught animals and wooden ploughs were given to those in need. The famine continued until the rains returned in 1985. However, despite the efforts of foreign relief agencies and governments, parts of Ethiopia were hit once more by famine when the rains failed in 1987. Much more long-term aid is needed if such famines are to become a thing of the past.

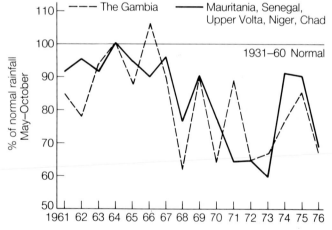

E Rainfall in W. African Sahel 1961–76

1 a Where is the Sahel?
b How many km long (east-west) and wide (north-south) is the Sahel drought zone?
c Study A. Use an atlas to name the countries in the Sahel affected by drought and famine.
d How many people live in these countries altogether (see B)?
2 a Look at D. The number of dry months (below 25 mm) has been omitted. Draw your own table and fill in the dry months for each region of West Africa.
b Describe the climate and vegetation of the Sahel.

c What happened to the amount of rainfall after 1968?
3 a What is nomadic pastoralism? Why is it so common in the Sahel?
b What is bush fallowing? Why is the fallow period necessary?
c Why were the Sahel countries forced to rely on foreign aid?
4 a Make a list of the factors you consider contributed to the Sahel famine. Try to put them in order of importance.
b Go through your list and suggest what solutions (if any) could be introduced to prevent those factors from causing another famine.
c Why are food handouts not the best long-term answer to a famine?

26 : Watering the Desert

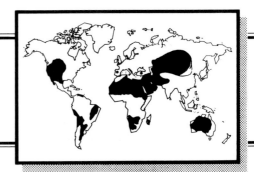

BY THEIR VERY NATURE, deserts receive inadequate rainfall to support much human, animal or plant life. Very few deserts are fortunate enough to have other water sources, though some have major rivers flowing through them eg the Nile in Egypt, the Colorado in the USA, the Indus in Pakistan. Yet the deserts can be made to bloom if water is provided.

The amount of water required depends on the prevailing temperature and resultant evaporation loss, the type of crop grown and the kind of soil.

Traditional Methods   The watering of dry or arid lands, known as **irrigation**, has been practised for thousands of years. Even today, the same traditional methods using human or animal muscle power to lift water from rivers and wells are in common use.

The water is usually sent to the fields along narrow canals or ditches, then diverted along furrows between the rows of crops (**B**). The amount of water can be controlled simply by blocking the end of the furrows with a mound of earth. If there is a river nearby, water can be led off from the river or stored behind small dams when it floods. However, this method cannot provide water all year round.

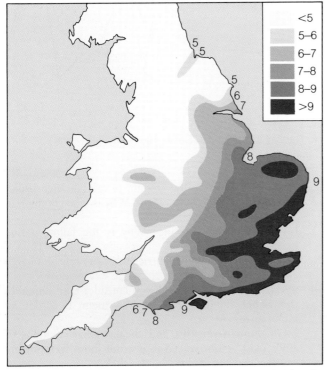

	<5
	5–6
	6–7
	7–8
	8–9
	>9

A Average number of years per decade when irrigation is likely to be necessary in England and Wales

B Furrow irrigation in southern California

Modern Methods   Dams have been used for a very long time to store water in man-made lakes called **reservoirs**. With the invention of modern machines and materials, especially concrete, the number and size of dams in the world has jumped dramatically. Giant diggers can excavate canals hundreds of kilometres in length and line them with concrete. Tunnels can also be bored through mountains. This means that suitable valleys far from the source of water can now be irrigated.

Many desert areas have been found to lie above huge underground **aquifers**. These are layers of rock which have soaked up rainfall over thousands of years. Particularly important are **permeable** rocks such as sandstone, chalk or limestone which allow water to pass easily through them. This water can be allowed to rise to the surface under its own pressure in **artesian wells**, or it can be pumped.

Water is still spread over the fields by the traditional furrow method, but modern methods are less wasteful of water. These include overhead sprinklers (**D**), rotating water jets that throw out the water in a circle, or irrigation pipes laid on the surface of the soil.

Problems
- Salinity. Desert soils are often salty. When water is added, the salts dissolve, but they rise and build up at the surface when the water evaporates. These salts can kill the crops. The only answer is to lay expensive drainage pipes beneath the fields to remove the salt, but then there is the problem of where to discharge these drainage pipes.
- Waterlogging. The addition of too much water to flat, low-lying areas can make the soil waterlogged.

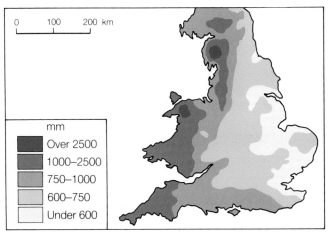

0   100   200 km

mm

■	Over 2500
■	1000–2500
■	750–1000
■	600–750
□	Under 600

C Average annual rainfall in England and Wales

- Removing too much water from aquifers results in a fall in the water table. Pumping becomes more difficult and expensive. Eventually the water may be used up.
- Pumping of fresh water from wells near coasts can enable salt water to invade the rock and soil. As a result, the land becomes useless for farming.
- Water may carry diseases. Insects such as mosquitos breed in the stagnant water, causing the spread of malaria. In Africa, a water snail spreads the worm which causes bilharzia or 'river blindness'.
- Extraction of underground water can cause the land to subside.

D Irrigation by overhead sprinklers

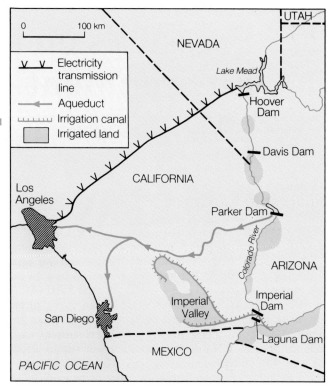

V V Electricity
        transmission
        line
——← Aqueduct
⊔⊔⊔⊔ Irrigation canal
▨ Irrigated land

E Uses of the Colorado River, USA

F Some Major Irrigation Schemes

Country	River	Main Dams
Egypt	Nile	Aswan
USA	Colorado	Hoover, Parker, Imperial
USA	Columbia	Grand Coulee
USA	Sacramento	Shasta
Pakistan	Indus	Sukkur, Kotri
Australia	Murray/ Murrumbidgee	Tumut
South Africa	Orange	Vaal Hartz
Ghana	Volta	Akosombo
USSR	Dnieper	Kakhovka, Zaporazhe
USSR	Volga	Volgograd
China	Hwang Ho	Sanmenxia

1 Write a sentence to explain the meaning of each of these terms:
   a permeable **b** aquifer **c** artesian well **d** water table **e** irrigation

2 **a** With the help of an atlas, locate the major irrigation schemes listed in **F** on an outline map of the world.
   b What do you notice about their distribution?

3 **a** Explain what is meant by furrow irrigation.
   b What modern methods are replacing furrow irrigation?
   c Why is furrow irrigation being replaced?

4 **a** Study **A** and **C**. Which regions are most likely to need irrigation?
   b Suggest why irrigation is needed in these regions.
   c Which method of irrigation is most likely? Give reasons for your answer.

5 **a** Many irrigation schemes are part of multi-purpose projects. Study **E**. What are the uses of the Hoover Dam project?
   b Suggest why the Colorado River is only a trickle when it enters the sea.
   c What are the problems likely to be faced by water authorities when a river like the Colorado has many uses and crosses several state and national boundaries? How might these problems be overcome?

6 Explain why irrigation is not always a success in arid regions.

27 : Pressures on the Environment

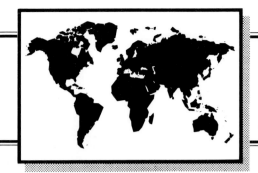

Spaceship Earth

PLANET EARTH is like a spaceship. It carries a crew of around 5,000 million people together with all of the oxygen, food and raw materials that they need to survive and prosper. But another 1,000 million people will have to be fed, clothed, houses and employed by the year 2000 (**A**).

All over the world, fuels and minerals such as coal or oil are being taken from the ground faster than they can be replaced by nature. These **non-renewable resources** took millions of years to form, but may disappear within a few decades (**D**). Other resources such as wood, cotton or wool are **renewable** since we can grow more of them to meet demand in a relatively short time.

There are several possible reactions to this pressure on resources:

- make more efficient use of existing sources of water, land and minerals eg more intensive farming, dam building, terracing hillsides, recycling scrap.
- seek out new resources in areas not previously explored or exploited eg oil and gas in Alaska and Siberia, bauxite in the Amazon.
- slow down the population growth rate.
- replace scarce or expensive resources with new substitutes eg synthetic rubber, plastics, manmade fibres.

Pressure for Change

This depends on three main factors:
- **The population pressure** As **B** shows, the world's people are not evenly spread. People are attracted by such factors as a warm, moist climate and fertile soil. They tend to avoid places with extremes of temperature and lack of water or other useful resources.

    As long as the supply of local resources is sufficient to enable the population to grow and thrive, there is little pressure to migrate. In the past, when population

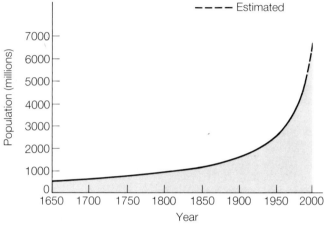

A World population growth 1650–2000

pressure became too great, people simply moved to 'empty' lands. In the Middle Ages, for example, groups such as the Mongols and Vikings migrated thousands of kilometres in search of new land and a better environment. Sparsely inhabited continents such as North America and Australia were settled by Europeans during the migrations of the 19th century.

- **The demand for resources** Modern society depends on an unending supply of water, food, fuel and raw materials. In order to provide these, multinational corporations and governments are prepared to spend huge sums of money on exploring and opening up the few remaining untouched regions. As a result, people are now moving into inhospitable areas such as Siberia, Alaska and the Amazon rainforest. Unfortunately, the balance of nature is often upset by such sudden, drastic change.

- **The level of technology used by the society** In the poorer countries of the world, life for the farmers and villagers has changed little in the last 100 years. Traditional methods of farming, using manual labour or animals, only change the environment slowly (**E**).

Region	Area (000 sq. km)	% of total	Population (millions)	% of total	Pop. density per sq. km
Africa	30,330	22	601	11.9	19.8
North America	21,515	16	270	5.4	12.5
Latin America	20.566	15	421	8.4	20.5
Asia (excluding USSR)	27,576	20	2,930	58.3	106.3
Europe (excluding USSR)	4,937	4	495	9.8	100.3
USSR	22,408	17	284	5.7	12.7
Oceania	8,510	6	25	0.5	2.9

B World population – 1987 estimates

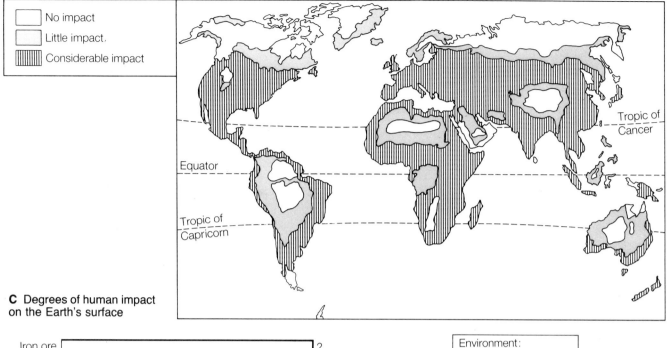

▢	No impact
▨	Little impact,
▥	Considerable impact

C Degrees of human impact on the Earth's surface

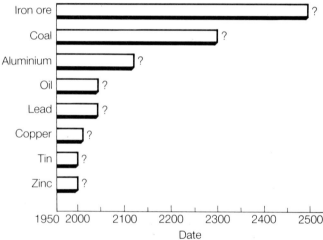

D Estimated lifetimes of world mineral resources

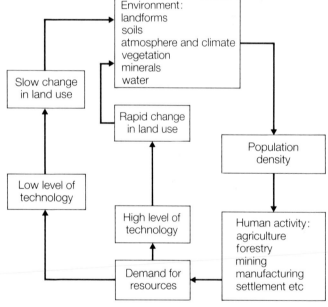

E Human activity and the natural environment

In advanced countries where machines replace manpower, the rate of change is many times faster. Great rivers can be tamed or diverted; whole forests can be destroyed; deserts can bloom as irrigation water is brought over hundreds of kilometres. The natural environment is altered into an unrecognisable man-made landscape.

1 a Look at **E**. What is meant by the term 'environment'?
b What are non-renewable resources? Give an example.
c What are renewable resources? Give an example.
d Study **D**. Assuming you live to the age of 70, which resources are expected to run out during your lifetime?
e Suggest why the resource lifetimes shown in **D** are uncertain.

2 a Explain the meaning of the term 'population density'.
b Using the statistics in **B**, draw a bar graph to show the population densities of the different regions.
c Which regions do you think are possibly underpopulated in relation to their land area?

3 a Find a world population density map in an atlas. Which parts of the world appear to be densely populated? Which parts of the world are sparsely populated?
b Look at **C**. In which parts of the world has there been little or no human impact?
c Suggest reasons why the areas named in **b** are hardly affected by human activity. An atlas may help.
d In which group is your country shown in **C**? Do you agree with this? Give reasons for your answer.

4 What are the three main factors which influence the rate of environmental change caused by human activity?

28 : Ecosystems

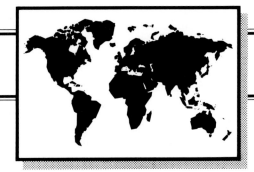

WHEN A NUMBER of separate parts fit together and affect or influence each other, they all become part of a **system**. All living things exist in close relationship with each other and with their physical environment. This interaction between plants, animals or people and the local relief, climate, soil and vegetation takes place within an **ecosystem**. Different ecosystems can be found in woodlands, streams, farms or even cities, but the nature of each ecosystem depends on:

- Its energy inputs and outputs. In nature, energy usually comes from the sun. It is used by plants during **photosynthesis** to help them grow. However, people also add energy through their work and use of machines.
- The supply of nutrients or plant foods. This depends on the type of soil, which in turn depends on many factors such as climate, relief, parent rock and natural vegetation. Nutrients are returned to the soil from dead organic matter by **decomposers** such as insects and bacteria.

- The population of plants and animals. Ecosystems such as the tropical rainforest support many different species because they can rapidly cycle their supplies of energy and nutrients.

Food Chains Energy in an ecosystem is passed on to animals when they eat plants, and then to larger flesh-eating animals (**carnivores**) when they eat the plant-eaters (**herbivores**). Some energy is lost at each stage as the plants and animals use it up simply to stay alive. The result is a **food chain** with many plants and small insects or animals at the bottom, and a few large carnivores at the top (**B**). When a number of food chains overlap, they are known as a **food web**.

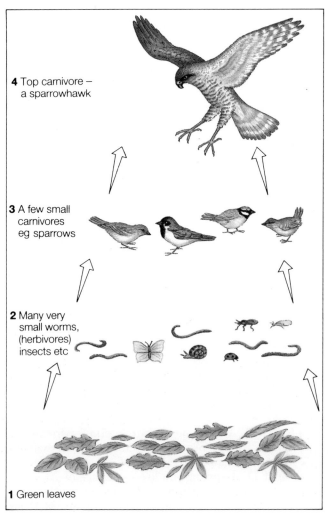

A Simplified circulation of nutrients and energy in an ecosystem

B A simple food chain pyramid

58

Chemicals In The Environment

A vast range of chemicals is added to the environment every day. These include many poisons such as:

- **insecticides** which are intended to kill insects which attack crops or carry diseases such as malaria;
- **herbicides** which kill weeds;
- **fungicides** which kill fungi on crops.

These chemicals increase farmers' harvests and profits. They also help save people's lives: in India alone, the use of DDT against mosquitoes reduced the number of malaria cases from 75 million to 5 million in just 10 years. But insects eventually become resistant to the chemicals if they are overused. Such chemicals can linger for years in the soil or be washed into streams and lakes, where they affect marine life. The poisons pass up the food chain, being stored in the bodies of animals and humans and presenting a serious health risk (**D**). The use of DDT has now been banned in many countries.

D DDT residues from NE USA (1967)

Source	Concentration (ppm)
Water	0.00005
Plankton	0.040
Shrimp	0.16
Mud snail	0.26
Flying insects	0.30
Minnow	0.94
Duck	1.07
Flounder	1.28
Grass roots	2.80
Common tern	3.42
Osprey	13.8
Herring gull	18.5
Cormorant	26.4
Ring billed gull	75.5

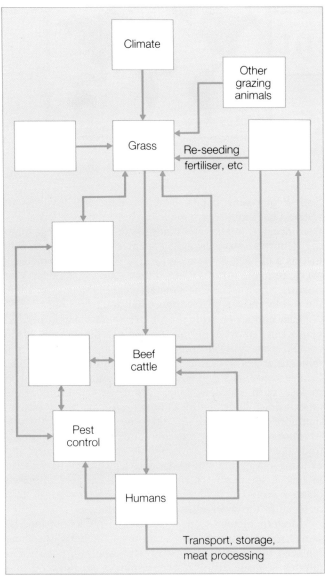

C A simplified grass-beef-humans ecosystem

The Balancing Act

Ecosystems are usually delicately balanced, though they can change over long periods of time, perhaps when new plants or animals arrive, or the climate changes. However, the natural balance can easily be upset by human activity.

In most of the populated parts of the world, natural vegetation has been cleared. Fire is often used for this clearance. Many experts believe that the savanna grasslands of tropical Africa are not natural, but the result of regular burning and grazing over several thousand years. Grasses quickly grow after a fire, while trees are killed or take a long time to recover.

When trees are cut down or grass is ploughed up for agriculture, the natural ecosystem is destroyed. The nutrients which were returned to the soil by dead leaves or roots no longer exist and have to be replaced by fertiliser or manure. The protection given by continuous plant cover from rain and wind no longer exists, so erosion becomes a problem. As plants are cleared and animals are killed, food chains are disrupted.

1 Write a sentence explaining the meaning of each of these terms:
   a ecosystem **b** decomposer **c** carnivore **d** herbivore
2 **a** Describe what **B** shows.
   b Why is the food chain in **B** a pyramid shape?
   c What do you think would happen to this food chain if the sparrowhawks were all killed?
   d What do you think would happen to this food chain if the trees were cleared for arable (crop) farming?
   e Draw a simple food chain with yourself at the top.
   f Explain the different DDT residues listed in **D**.
   g Why were chemicals like DDT first introduced?
   h Why has DDT been banned in many countries in recent years?
3 **a** Study **A**. Explain how each part of a simple ecosystem is inter-related.
   b Copy **C**. Complete the flow diagram using these five labels in the correct boxes: (i) soil (ii) plant diseases (iii) selective breeding (iv) animal diseases (v) fossil fuel energy.
   c How could this grass-beef-humans ecosystem be upset? Give reasons for your answer.

29 : Soil Development

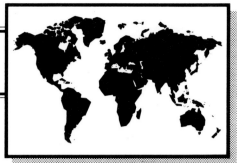

WHEN WE WALK across a field, one of the world's most valuable resources, often no more than a metre deep, lies just beneath our feet – the soil. Soil is an essential part of our food supply system. Without it there would be no crops and no animal or human life on Earth.

What Is Soil?   Soil comes from two main sources. Most of it is weathered bedrock, but an important part comes from rotting plant and animal matter. The type of soil also depends on age, slope, climate and natural vegetation.

Weathered rock contains particles of different sizes (**A**). These may include large pebbles such as flint or gravel, but the most important particles are sand, silt and clay (in order of decreasing size). They can be separated by a simple test. Rub damp soil between your fingers. If it feels rough and does not stick together, it contains a lot of sand. Silt and clay both feel smooth but silt does not stick together, while clay can be rolled into threads.

The larger particles fit so loosely together that large spaces or **pores** allow water to infiltrate rapidly through sand or gravel. Clay particles are so small (less than 0.002 mm) that they pack closely together, preventing easy movement of water through the soil (**B**). Clay is therefore **impermeable**.

Soil Processes   Plants feed on minerals dissolved in water. These minerals come from the weathered bedrock or from decayed animal and plant matter. When living things die, nature's waste disposal system comes into operation: insects and bacteria break down the dead leaves which fall every autumn, turning them into a dark surface layer of **humus** which is rich in minerals. This is then mixed into the soil by insects, worms and other animals (**C**).

Clay particles tend to hold onto minerals chemically, but plants can remove the minerals and use them. Soils which contain clay and minerals are said to be **fertile**. Soil minerals are easily washed out or **leached** from many soils. Coarse sandy soils which receive large amounts of rain tend to lose most of their minerals due to water infiltrating quickly down to the bedrock and into streams. Such soils are therefore **infertile** and are said to be **acid**.

Poor soils can be improved by adding minerals. This was traditionally done by mixing in lime or animal manure, and by using a crop rotation. Crops such as wheat or barley tend to take a lot of minerals out of soil. Farmers therefore planted crops such as clover, peas or beans which trap nitrogen in the soil and restore the fertility.

Modern intensive farming often involves growing the same crop year after year. Traditional methods are being replaced by chemical fertilisers – phosphates, potash and nitrates – made from scarce resources such as oil and natural gas in giant chemical plants. Some experts are worried because these destroy the soil structure, reduce the capacity to hold water and are easily leached.

1   Write a sentence explaining each of these terms:
a acid soil **b** leaching **c** fertile soil **d** humus
2   **a** What are the two main sources of soil material?
b What other factors influence soil type?
c How would you recognise sand, silt or clay soils?
d Study **B**. What are the differences between sand and clay soils? Explain these differences.
e What name is given in **A** to a soil which is a mixture of sand, silt and clay?
f How will the characteristics of such a soil compare with sand or clay soils? Why do many farmers prefer it over the other types?
3   **a** Draw or trace **C**. Complete the diagram using the correct numbers for the labels on the key.
b Describe the processes taking place in a typical soil.

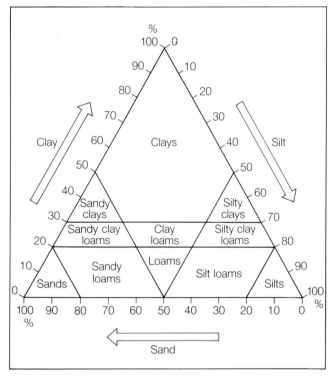

A Soil texture diagram based on size of inorganic particles

60

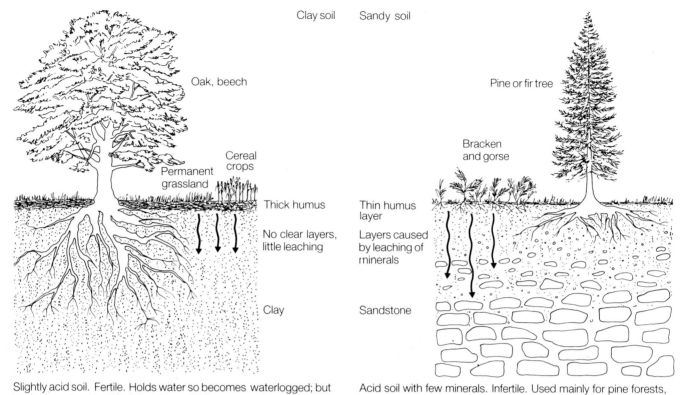

Clay soil   Sandy soil

Oak, beech

Pine or fir tree

Permanent grassland

Cereal crops

Bracken and gorse

Thick humus

Thin humus layer

No clear layers, little leaching

Layers caused by leaching of minerals

Clay

Sandstone

Slightly acid soil. Fertile. Holds water so becomes waterlogged; but hard when dry. Used for intensive agriculture – cereals or permanent grass for cattle.

Acid soil with few minerals. Infertile. Used mainly for pine forests, heathland, building or recreation.

B Soils found on clay and sandstone bedrocks

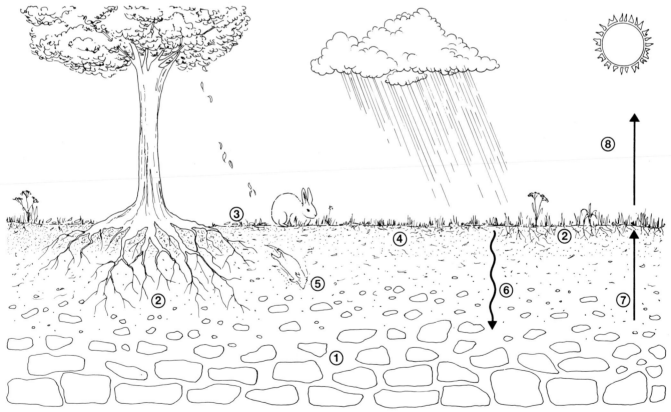

Soil mixed and aerated by worms, moles, etc.
Roots take up minerals from soil
Water evaporated from surface
Leaves fall to ground
Minerals washed down by rainwater

Weathered bedrock releases minerals
Soil moisture drawn towards surface
Dead animal and vegetable matter decays into humus and releases minerals

C Soil processes

30 : Soil Erosion

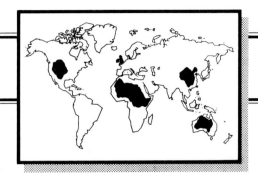

SOIL IS very slow to form but can very quickly be removed. Rates of soil renewal in Britain range between 0.2 and 1 tonne per hectare per year. At this rate it takes several centuries for a new layer of soil 1 cm thick to form. Yet soil is being eroded all over the world at many times this rate. The problem is that erosion is often not obvious. A farm losing 100 tonnes of soil per hectare per year loses less than 1 cm depth of soil per year.

Causes of Soil Erosion

Soil is usually blown away by the wind or washed away by surface runoff. Under a cover of permanent grass or woodland, there is hardly any erosion, but the situation changes when land is cleared for arable farming. Once the soil is ploughed and prepared for cultivation, it is bare and exposed to wind and water.

Periods of dry weather and strong wind can cause large amounts of fine topsoil to blow away like a desert sandstorm (**A**). Modern farms have large fields and few hedges or trees to act as windbreaks. In Britain, the soils most at risk from the wind are the loamy sands of East Anglia, Nottinghamshire and the Vale of York, and the peats of the Fens. In the drier climates of Australia, Africa, China and the Dust Bowl of the USA, the risks are much greater.

Heavy raindrops strike with enough force to move soil particles on even gentle slopes (**B**). Yet in recent years, crop farming has spread onto ever steeper slopes, such as the chalk downland of southern England, as farmers try to earn more money from their land.

Once the soil is saturated, surface runoff begins. A sheet of water collects on the surface and moves downhill, often concentrating in crop rows or in hard, compacted ruts caused by heavy farm machinery. Farmers who work the land up and down slope provide man-made rills which collect runoff and accelerate erosion. These may soon turn into deep gulleys.

B A raindrop striking bare soil

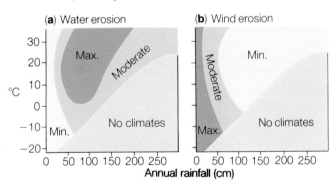

C Rates of soil erosion due to running water and wind under different climatic conditions

On rolling land, soil is removed more rapidly from hilltops and steep slopes than from the gentle ones lower down. As soil becomes thinner on the valley sides, it becomes deeper in the valley bottom. Some of the soil will be carried into rivers and deposited some distance downstream. This may cause river blockages and more flooding.

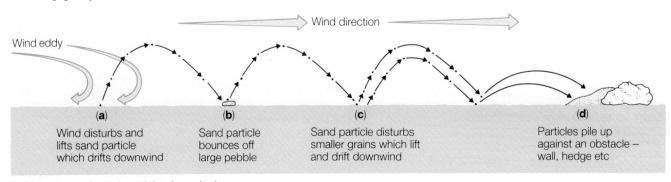

A Movement of sand particles by saltation

D Soil erosion in Ethiopia

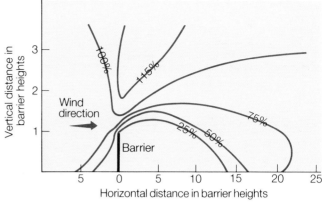

E The effect of a wind break (normal wind speed = 100%)

Afforestation (the planting of trees) is most effective on steep slopes. Another method commonly used in south-east Asia, where flat land is scarce, is to create **terraces** or steps in the hillside. These collect runoff and eroded soil, and help prevent soil creep.

The only long-term solution to erosion is education. Farmers must adapt methods and crops to fit in with the local environment rather than simply seek the fastest profit.

Solutions

The most effective answer is to provide a blanket of vegetation for as long as possible. Plants protect the soil from wind and rain, and their roots hold the soil together.

On flatter land, **contour ploughing** and **strip farming** are used. Instead of ploughing and planting up and down slope, farmers work the land across the slope, following the contours. Increasing the surface roughness by careful ploughing can slow down the wind. Alternating rows or strips of different crops also reduce the effects of wind and runoff. Walls, hedges and lines of trees act as wind breaks. They reduce wind speed (**E**) and enable any eroded soil to collect at their base. Keeping soil fairly moist also reduces wind erosion.

1 **a** Study **C**. What are the climatic conditions which most favour i) wind erosion ii) erosion by running water?
   b Which type of erosion is most likely in Britain?
2 **a** What type of erosion is shown in **D**?
   b Give reasons for your answer.
3 **a** Explain the process of saltation (**A**).
   b Explain what **E** shows.
   c Why does a hedge, wall or line of trees help prevent soil erosion?
   d Make a list of any other methods used to reduce soil erosion.
   e Which methods of soil conservation are most useful in
   ● upland areas ● dry plains?
   f Briefly explain how each method shown in **F** works.

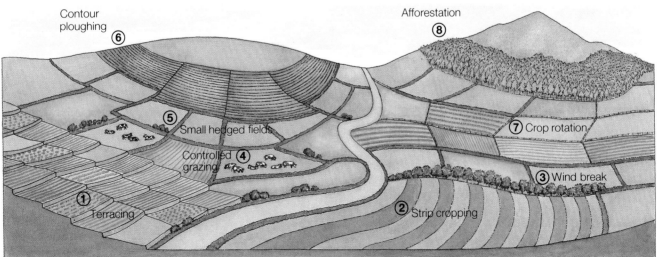

F Methods of soil conservation

31 : Creating a Dust Bowl

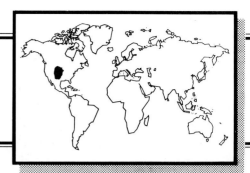

ON THE MORNING of 11 May, 1934, the people of Boston, Massachusetts, stopped in the streets to look up at the dirty, yellow sky. Thick dust hid the sun. Millions of tonnes of fine soil from the Great Plains of the USA were being blown into the Atlantic Ocean. This was the beginning of the drought which created a dust bowl from one sixth of the nation's land (A).

Settling the Plains Until the late 19th century, the Great Plains were regarded by settlers as 'The Great American Desert'. The rolling, treeless plains were inhabited only by small numbers of Indians who hunted vast herds of bison.

Things began to change when the railway came in 1868. Within a few years the bison were almost wiped out by hunters and railway construction men. The Indians and bison were replaced by cowboys and cattle which were sent by rail to the eastern markets.

During the 1870's, the first settlers arrived. Ranching was threatened by people arriving to plough up the grass on free land donated by the government. These **homesteaders** were given 64 hectares in exchange for living on the land and cultivating it. After 5 years, the land was theirs.

Two inventions ensured the farmers' victory by the late 1880's. The first of these was barbed wire, which provided material for fences in a region which lacked wood or stone. The other invention was the windpump which brought up underground water for irrigation and drinking.

The Hostile Environment The first homesteaders mostly came from the wetter lands of northern Europe. Their square, open fields and deep ploughing were not suited to the dry plains where wind and heavy rain could easily erode the fine, crumbly chernozem soil (B).

Apart from unreliable rainfall, the farmers had to contend with sub-zero temperatures in winter, blizzards, frost, hail and plagues of grasshoppers. In good years, half the crop succeeded; in the worst years, all the crops failed.

Wheat was the main crop of the plains. It needed good, reliable rainfall and was mostly sown in spring. This meant that the light, crumbly soils were exposed to erosion by strong winds. Erosion was also increased in fields left fallow to recover their fertility.

- - - - State boundary	▦ Heavy erosion
——— National boundary	▦ Moderate erosion
·········· 500 mm Isohyet	

A The Dust Bowl and the Great Plains of the USA

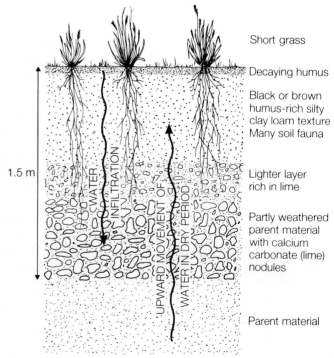

Short grass

Decaying humus

Black or brown humus-rich silty clay loam texture
Many soil fauna

Lighter layer rich in lime

Partly weathered parent material with calcium carbonate (lime) nodules

Parent material

B A chernozem soil found in the Great Plains

C The Dust Bowl of the Southern Plains, 1937

When the rains failed in the 1930s and the wheat failed to grow, huge amounts of fine topsoil were removed by the wind. Wells and streams went dry, cattle and sheep died of thirst, dust filled houses and stopped machinery, and tens of thousands of people abandoned home and moved away (**C**).

The Response Some farmers stayed on despite the drought. They learned how to reduce erosion by introducing more mixed farming and crop rotation instead of fallowing. In places, row crops like wheat have been replaced by permanent grass, with terraces cut into hillsides, strip-cropping and contour ploughing. Ponds and dams also hold the precious water.

The effects of wind have also been reduced by planting trees as wind breaks. Drought-resistant varieties of wheat ensure a harvest in all but the driest years, and straw is left on the surface after harvesting to protect the soil. Despite spending $45 billion between 1950–80, however, the position is little better today. One quarter of all US cropland loses at least two tonnes of soil per hectare per year. Farmers will not practice soil conservation until they can see the financial benefits. They continue to use intensive methods and grow crops on unsuitable land in times of more plentiful rainfall and high prices guaranteed by the government.

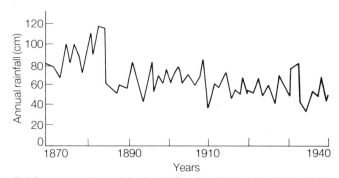

D Mean annual precipitation in Omaha, Nebraska 1870–1940

1 **a** With the help of an atlas, name the states most affected by the dust bowl problem of the 1930s.
   b What was the size of the area affected?
   c Why were the Great Plains once known as 'The Great American Desert'?
   d Study **C**. Why is wind erosion always a threat in this landscape?
2 **a** Study **D**. Which years recorded the highest and lowest precipitation for Omaha in Nebraska 1870–1940? What were the recorded figures?
   b What is the average annual precipitation for Omaha?

c Study your answers to **a** and **b**. What do these figures suggest was a major problem for farmers on the plains?
d Study **E**. Which are the hottest and wettest seasons on the plains? Why does this cause a problem for farmers?
e Most wheat is sown in autumn or spring. What problems arise from this timing?
f Study **B**. Is the chernozem soil likely to be acid and infertile? Give reasons for your answer (see unit 29).
g Why is a chernozem soil likely to suffer from erosion if the grass cover is removed?
3 **a** Divide the history of settlement on the plains into five periods.
   b For each period, state whether the local people and their way of life were well adapted to the plains ecosystem. Give reasons for your answers.
4 Write a brief summary of the reasons why soil conservation methods have not been as successful as hoped since the 1930s.

Fig. E Mean climatic figures for Omaha, Nebraska

Omaha	J	F	M	A	M	J	J	A	S	O	N	D	Total
Temp °C	−5.6	−4.4	2.8	10.6	17.2	22.2	25.0	23.9	18.9	12.8	3.9	−2.8	
Prec (mm)	18	23	33	71	104	119	102	81	76	58	28	23	736

32 : The Disappearing Forest

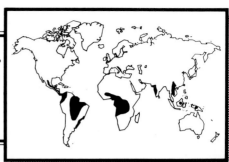

TROPICAL FORESTS (**A**) make up about one third of Earth's forest area, but they are so dense that they contain four fifths of the total world vegetation. They also contain half of all known wild creatures. More than 1 billion (1,000,000,000) people depend on rainforest watersheds. Yet today they are under threat from human development. Already, Latin America and Asia have lost 40%, and Africa over 50%, of their original forests. Some estimates suggest that over 20 million hectares are destroyed annually (an area almost equal to the United Kingdom).

Amazonia The world's largest rainforest is found in the Amazon river basin and lies mostly in Brazil. Until recently, the forest was largely uninhabited except along the river banks. In 1834, the total population of the region was estimated at nearly 150,000, over half of whom were Portuguese settlers. The largest town, Manaus, thrived in the rubber boom from 1870-1910, but interest died in Amazonia when rubber planting started in the Far East.

Today there is a new boom based on rich mineral deposits, timber, agriculture and industry. More than a million new jobs are being created in a country with high unemployment and poverty. The population of Amazonia is now 6 million and settlers are flocking to the Amazon along a new road system. Many are squatters who cannot afford to buy land. Life is hard: the soil is poor, diseases are widespread, there are few basic services such as electricity or clean, piped water, and life expectancy is low. However, billions of pounds are being invested in huge projects by the government, the World Bank, and by foreign companies. By 1983, more than 700 projects had been approved. Many of these are related to the Polamazonia Plan (**F**). This will involve mining of various metals, and construction of several aluminium smelters, an electric railway, a fertiliser plant, two river ports, and the fourth largest dam in the world.

B Deforestation by subsistence farmers

Activity	Area affected per year
Commercial logging	45,000 sq. km.
Fuelwood gathering	25,000 sq. km.
Ranching	20,000 sq. km.
Shifting cultivation	160,000 sq. km.
Mining, roads, dams etc.	100,000 sq. km.?

C Destruction of rainforests (1984)

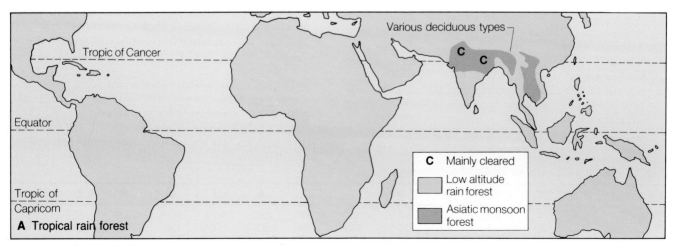

A Tropical rain forest

(a) Before development

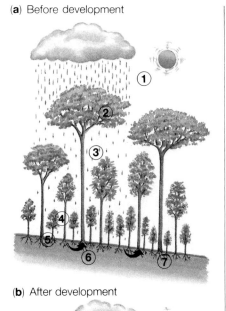

(1) Hot, wet climate all year

(2) Broad tree crowns block rain and heat

(3) Light spray drips to forest floor

(4) Dense shade – little undergrowth

(5) Thick leaf litter

(6) Minerals from decayed plants and leaves taken up by roots

(7) Thick soil

(b) After development

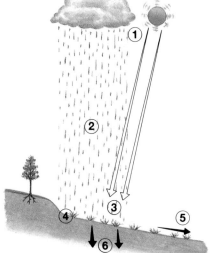

(1)

(2)

(3)

(4)

(5)

(6)

D The effects of human clearance on tropical rainforest

Shifting Cultivation. People in the more remote tropical forest areas survive by a combination of hunting, gathering and shifting cultivation. They live in temporary homes. This subsistence farming system is adapted to the infertile clay soil which is leached daily by heavy rainfall. Clearings are made in the forest by cutting down the trees and by burning (**B**) Wood ash acts as a fertiliser, but it does not last long and there are no animals for manure. Little time is spent tending the crops of rice, tapioca, yams, maize or cassava. After two or three years the group abandons the clearing to start again nearby. The forest slowly returns, but if the population grows quickly, the land is reused too soon for its fertility to revive.

??? ? ? ? ? ?

1 **a** Copy **A** onto an outline map of the world. With the help of an atlas, label these regions: Amazon, Congo (Zaire), India, Indonesia.
b Study **E**. Why are climatic conditions ideal for the growth of dense rainforest?

2 **a** Copy **D**. Add these labels to fit the key for **D** b.

Rain falls on unprotected ground   No leaf litter
Rainfall decreases   Rapid soil erosion
Soil minerals   Sun bakes bare soil
rapidly leached

b Suggest why the rainforest has limited use for agriculture.

3 **a** Draw a bar graph to show the information in **C**.
b What is meant by shifting cultivation?
c How is shifting cultivation adapted to the rainforest ecosystem?

4 **a** Why was Amazonia sparsely populated until recently?
b Why are new settlers coming to Amazonia?
c Many environmental groups oppose the development of Amazonia. Do you agree or disagree with them? Explain your viewpoint in as much detail as possible.

F The Polamazonia Plan

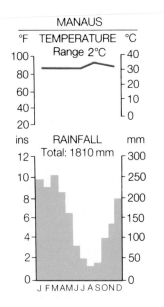

E Climate graph for Manaus in Amazonia

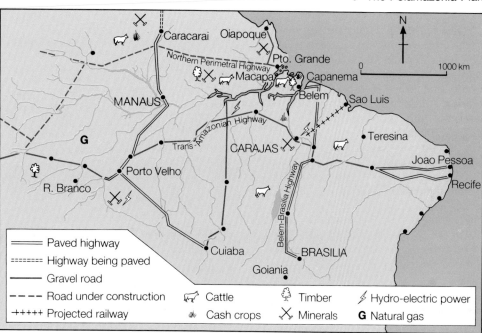

33 : Creating New Land

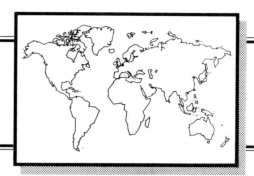

ANYONE who has sunk ankle deep into mud in a bog or marsh knows that river valleys or stretches of coast are not always 'dry land'. People have used these wetlands for hunting wildlife, fishing, collecting reeds and seasonal grazing over thousands of years. However, people have often regarded the wetlands as wasted when they could be used for intensive agriculture or building.

The Dutch Polders

The Netherlands are highly vulnerable to flooding. Most of the western Netherlands lie at or just below sea level. They would be flooded at high tide if there was no man-made protection (**B**).

2,000 years ago the western Netherlands consisted of marshes, bogs and shallow lakes. They were affected by sea tides and crossed by a shifting network of rivers, estuaries and creeks. The soil was fertile peat and clay. This encouraged the sparse population to protect small patches of land from flooding by building raised dykes around them. There were many disasters, but as the population increased and technical knowledge improved over the centuries, the entire area was reclaimed (**A**).

Draining the Marsh Dykes (embankments) were built from the 12th century onwards to protect low-lying silt from sea erosion. A similar method is still used in places: low dams are built in the sea to trap sand and mud which settle behind them.

The most important method, however, was introduced in the 17th century when windmills, canals and dykes were first used to drain lakes. Today, the windmills have been replaced by diesel and electrical pumping systems. The fertile land which is exposed by drainage is known as a **polder**. Many polders are five metres or more below sea level and only exist because of the system of dykes and drainage ditches.

The process begins with construction of a main dyke with a sandy core and covering of boulder clay. A road usually runs along the top of the dyke. Then the water behind the dyke is pumped out, the soil is analysed, and tile drains are laid. Water from these drains goes into polder ditches, then is pumped into a system of main ditches and canals which take it to the sea (**D** and **E**). While the first crops are being grown, roads, farms and villages are built for the first settlers.

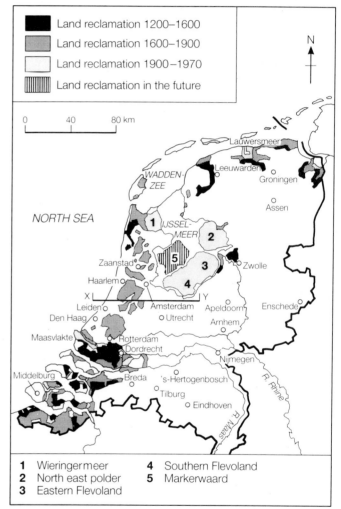

Land reclamation 1200–1600
Land reclamation 1600–1900
Land reclamation 1900–1970
Land reclamation in the future

0   40   80 km

1 Wieringermeer   4 Southern Flevoland
2 North east polder   5 Markerwaard
3 Eastern Flevoland

A Land reclamation in the Netherlands

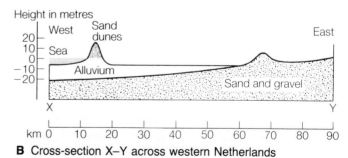

B Cross-section X–Y across western Netherlands

C Land reclamation in the Netherlands per century (sq. km)

Century	13th	14th	15th	16th	17th	18th	19th	20th
Land reclaimed	350	350	425	710	1120	500	1170	2300

The Zuyder Zee Project

The biggest challenge of recent times is the Zuyder Zee Project in the northern Netherlands. The Zuyder Zee was a large sea inlet which was a continual flood threat to nearby areas. A scheme was devised to drain much of the inlet and create five large polders. When completed in 1930, the first of these (Wieringermeer) provided 20,000 hectares of rich farmland. A 30 km long barrier dam was built in 1932, creating a freshwater lake and improving communications. Three more polders followed, covering 145,000 hectares.

The entire polderland has been laid out according to a detailed plan. The early polders were mainly intended for arable farming, but planners now use them to reduce population pressure in the rest of the country. Land has been set aside in the newer polders for recreation, forestry, industry and urban settlement. Each polder has its hierarchy of new settlements ranging from individual farms to villages, small towns and one main town. In addition, a new central town called Lelystad has been built to take overspill population from Amsterdam. It is a route and service centre for the entire region.

1   **a** What is the meaning of the word reclamation?
    b Why is land reclaimed only in the western Netherlands?
    c What forms a natural barrier protecting the Netherlands from the sea?
    d Study **C**. Draw a bar graph to show land reclaimed per century.
    e In which century was most land reclaimed? Why?

2   **a** Explain these terms: ● polder, ● dyke.
    b How is water removed from a polder?
    c Explain the stages in polder reclamation.
    d Describe a typical polder landscape.

3   **a** Explain why the Zuyder Zee Project was begun.
    b What are the main features of the Zuyder Zee Project?

4   There has been a long debate in Netherlands about whether to drain Markerwaard, the fifth Zuyder Zee polder, at a cost of £600 million. What are the arguments for and against such large scale drainage and reclamation of wetlands?

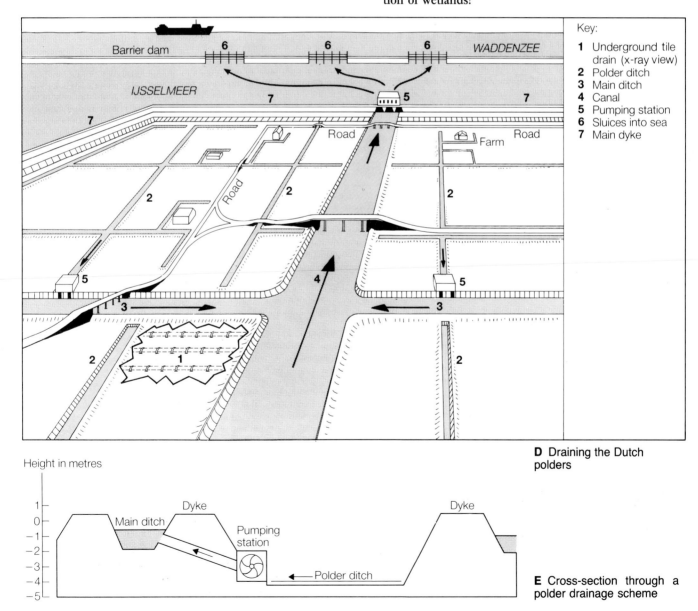

D Draining the Dutch polders

Key:
1 Underground tile drain (x-ray view)
2 Polder ditch
3 Main ditch
4 Canal
5 Pumping station
6 Sluices into sea
7 Main dyke

Height in metres

E Cross-section through a polder drainage scheme

34 : Changing the Countryside

BRITAIN'S COUNTRYSIDE is changing faster than at any time since the Agricultural Revolution more than 200 years ago. This is mainly the result of major changes in the rural economy.

The New Agricultural Revolution

About 80% of the land in Britain is used for farming. Forty years ago, most of this was improved grassland. Mixed farming was common, with cereals, fodder crops as animal feed, and livestock which provided manure all on one farm. Today, many farmers, particularly on the flat, fertile land of eastern England, have changed to **monoculture** – specialised cultivation of one crop. The aim of such **intensive** farming is to produce the highest yield from each hectare.

Modern agriculture is very much like a business. This **agribusiness** involves borrowing money from a bank to pay for new machines, sheds and other improvements which increase harvests and profits. The spread of machines such as tractors and combine harvesters has meant that few farm workers are now required. Today, less than 3% of the working population is employed in agriculture.

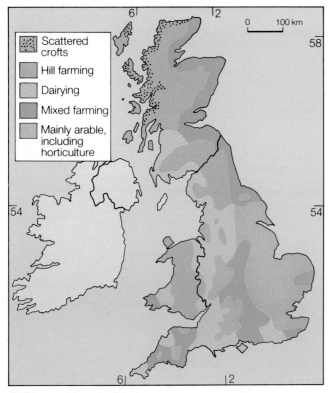

A Types of farm in Britain

 SON

 FATHER

- I like hedgerows. They shelter the fields and animals and protect wildlife.
- We don't need workers or tied cottages now – just the family and a new YTS trainee every year.
- New methods will give us bigger profits so we can soon pay off a bank loan.
- I like a mixed farm. They ensure a steady income and work all year.
- Muck spreading is better for the soil and avoids using expensive chemical fertilisers.

- I make a small profit and I don't owe any money to the bank.
- The new machines save us time and effort, and give us higher yields. We must have bigger fields for them.
- EEC subsidies make mixed farming out of date. We can make more money if we concentrate on one crop.
- The farm workers have always lived in the tied cottages and they've never let me down.
- Fertilisers and pesticides will give us higher yields.

B Attitudes in modern farming

Larger farms and fields are needed to use machines most efficiently and to avoid wasting valuable land. As a result, farmers have taken advantage of government subsidies to pull up hedges, fill in ponds, drain fens and wetlands, and plough up grass-covered downlands or moorland fringes. The increase in cropland and yields per hectare means that Britain now produces nearly two-thirds of its food requirements, compared with half in 1960. The cut in imported food and growth in exports saves Britain £2 billion a year.

The Food Mountains

A major cause of change in farming was Britain's joining the European Economic Community (EEC) in 1973. EEC policy has been to support the small farmers of France and Italy, and to boost harvests by guaranteeing stable prices for produce even in times of plenty. Surpluses are bought by the EEC and stored, ready for export or times of shortage.

Year	1930	1940	1950
No. of tractors	30,000	80,000	310,000
1960	**1970**	**1980**	**1985**
410,000	420,000	435,000	365,000

C Number of farm tractors in Britain

Farmers in western Europe reacted by borrowing more money, buying more equipment, specialising in the produce which gave highest profits and using every available hectare of land. The policy was so successful that huge surpluses or 'food mountains' built up. By the end of 1986 there were nearly 17 million tonnes of grain, 1.5 million tonnes of butter, 620,000 tonnes of beef and 150 million litres of wine in EEC storage. Storage costs alone added up to a staggering £2.8 billion.

Reducing the Mountains The EEC is now trying to cut back its spending by reducing production. Already, strict cutbacks have been made in dairying, causing some 2,500 British farmers to go out of business or sell their cattle. Meanwhile, the British government wants to convert 2 million hectares of farmland to other uses including recreation, forestry and building. The changes in the British countryside have not ended yet.

1 **a** Study **A**. Where in Britain is dairying most commonly found?
b What has happened to the area under improved grassland in England and Wales since 1947?
c Where in Britain is arable farming most commonly found?
d What has happened to the area under crops in England and Wales since 1947?
e What is mixed farming?
f Write a sentence to explain why mixed farming is less popular today than in 1947.
g Draw a line graph to show the statistics in **C**.
h Explain the changes shown on your graph.

2 Study **E**, then make a list of 10 changes which have taken place in the rural landscape in the last 40 years.

3 **a** **B** shows an imaginary conversation between a farmer and his son. The farmer wants to continue in the old ways while the son wants to introduce new ideas. Some comments are listed under the wrong person. Change the comments around so that they fit each person.
b With which person do you agree? Give reasons for your answer.

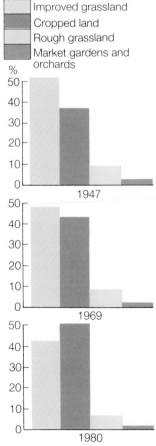

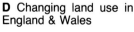

D Changing land use in England & Wales

E The changing English ▶ rural landscape

71

35 : Living with the Monsoon

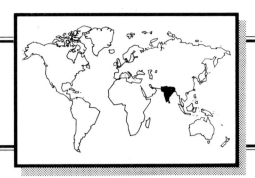

ABOUT ONE SEVENTH of the world's people live in India. By 1981, the Indian population had reached 684 million, an increase of more than 50% in just 20 years. Despite government efforts to promote birth control and smaller families, the population is still increasing by around 2% a year. As a result, increasing pressure is being placed on the country's environment and resources (**A**).

Agriculture in India   Three quarters of India's people still live in farms and villages. Most farms cover less than 3 ha, too small to provide sufficient food and income for a typical family. Many rural families rely on money from relatives with jobs in the cities.

Farmers are heavily dependent on the summer or south-west monsoon, a seasonal wind which brings 75% to 90% of India's rain within a period of 4 to 6 months (**B** and **C**). The rest of the year is dry, except in the extreme south. The monsoon is very unreliable – if the rains fail, people may starve. Irrigation is vital over most of India to provide water in the dry season, to give some protection against monsoon failure and to increase crop yields. Irrigated land produces twice as much grain as dry land, but only one third

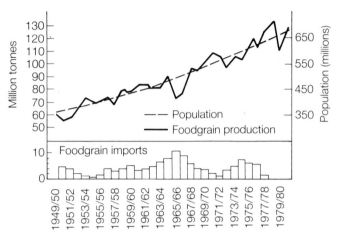

A India's population and food supply

of cropland is presently irrigated.

There are three main ways of storing water (**E**). Most of the main rivers have already been dammed for canal irrigation, particularly in the wide, fertile Ganges basin.

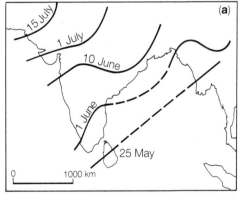

B The summer monsoon: average dates of **a** arrival **b** withdrawal

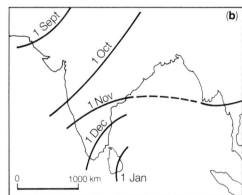

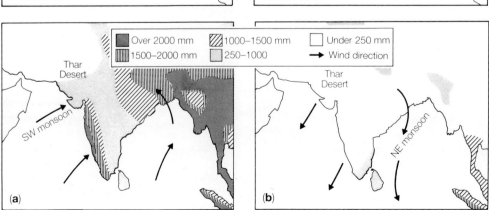

C Rainfall **a** May–October **b** November–April

D Rice farming in India

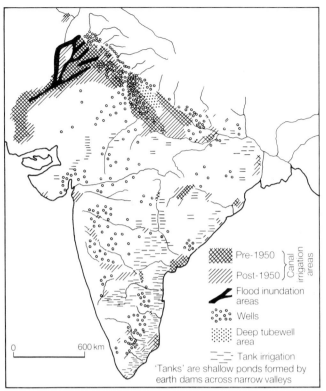

E Irrigation in India and Pakistan

Legend:
- Pre-1950 — Canal irrigation areas
- Post-1950 — Canal irrigation areas
- Flood inundation areas
- Wells
- Deep tubewell area
- Tank irrigation

'Tanks' are shallow ponds formed by earth dams across narrow valleys

0 — 600 km

Pressures On The Land Every year, agricultural land disappears under roads, houses, reservoirs and factories. If the Indian population continues to grow at the present rate, the area of land available to feed each person will drop from 0.33 ha in 1951 to 0.18 ha by the year 2000. This means that more food will have to be produced from less land.

In the attempt to produce more food, large areas of forest have been cut down. Marginal lands on steep slopes or desert fringes have been ploughed up or overgrazed. The result is serious soil erosion over one-sixth of the land area. Other problems arise from floods during the monsoon season, and from waterlogging and salinity (a surplus of salts) in the soil through careless use of irrigation.

The Green Revolution In the last 20 years, large-scale famine has disappeared in India, and a large grain store has been put aside for years of monsoon failure. This has been made possible by the introduction of high yielding varieties of wheat and rice, a process known as **The Green Revolution**. Yields of these crops have more than doubled in parts of the north.

Other high yielding varieties are being introduced eg maize and pulses. These will help continue the food surpluses for some time to come, but the population time bomb in India has still not been defused.

Bombay	J	F	M	A	M	J	J	A	S	O	N	D	
Temp °C	23	23	26	28	30	29	27	27	27	28	27	26	
Rain (mm)	2	2	2	2	18	486	618	340	246	64	13	2	1,808

F Mean monthly temperature and rainfall figures for Bombay (India)

1　a What is the monsoon?
　　b When does the south-west monsoon reach ● southern India ● north-west India?
　　c How long does the monsoon season last ● in the south ● in the north-west?
　　d Which parts of India receive most monsoon rain?
　　e Which parts of India are likely to suffer from drought?
2　a How much of India's cropland is currently irrigated?
　　b Name the three main methods of irrigation in India.
　　c Explain the differences between the three methods.

d Which method do you think is most expensive? Why?
e Which method do you think is least efficient? Why?
3　a What was the population increase in India between 1950 and 1981? (See **A**.)
　　b Use a calculator to work out India's population in the year 2000 if it continues to increase by 2% per annum.
　　c What was the Indian foodgrain production increase 1950–1980?
　　d What happened to foodgrain imports 1950–1980?
　　e Which major innovation caused this major improvement in India's food supply?
　　f India's population explosion creates many pressures on the environment. List four of these and give possible countermeasures.
4　Describe the similarities and differences between intensive farming in India and in Britain (see unit 34).

73

36 : Conservation or Development?

A Pressures on the Peak District National Park

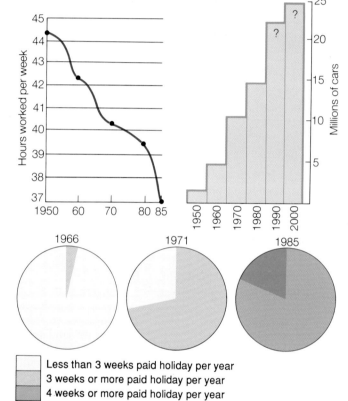

Less than 3 weeks paid holiday per year
3 weeks or more paid holiday per year
4 weeks or more paid holiday per year
5 weeks or more paid holiday per year

B Leisure in Britain

WHILE THE POPULATION of Britain has steadily increased, the length of time spent at work has steadily decreased . At the same time, the number of private cars has been increasing by up to 500,000 per year (**B**). People are now able to travel further and visit more remote areas in their leisure time. The result is an ever-growing pressure on the countryside, particularly the more scenic, less populated uplands.

Conservation Since the Second World War, governments have recognised the need to protect the countryside by careful control of new developments – a policy known as **conservation**. This involves limiting the damage caused to scenic landscapes by human activity such as mining, quarrying, farming, industry, erosion and pollution. It also means positive management of the countryside so that it can be more productive and benefit the whole nation. To achieve these aims, a number of protected areas have been set up by the government.

National Parks These were created in 1949 in order to:
• Preserve and improve the landscape.
• Provide facilities for public open air recreation.
• Preserve wildlife and historic buildings.
• Ensure a successful local economy.

Ten national parks were formed in England and Wales, all of them in the more remote upland areas of the north and the west. Most of the land remains in private hands, so public access is often restricted. Planning is usually controlled by local authorities, although there are independent planning boards in the Lake District and Peak District.

These boards monitor erosion and pollution. They also have powers to clear derelict sites, encourage tree planting, provide facilities for tourists and refuse permission for new developments. Despite this, permission has been given for mining, quarrying and large-scale industry within the Parks. In Scotland, the National Scenic Areas are similar to National Parks but less protected.

Other Conservation Areas There are many other areas in Britain which are protected in various degrees. **Country Parks** have been set up by local authorities to take pressure away from National Parks and Nature Reserves. They usually cover about 130 hectares and are often close to urban areas. This means they have to provide facilities for

C Land ownership in Peak District National Park (1987)

Private	70%
Forestry Commission	1%
Water authorities	13%
National Trust	10%
Local authorities + Peak Park Planning Board	6%

large numbers of visitors in a small area while giving a 'countryside experience'.

Areas of Outstanding Natural Beauty cover about 10% of England and Wales, but planning authorities have few powers to restrict farm, forestry or industrial development, and access for the public is very limited. A similar situation exists with the **Heritage Coasts** which cover more than 1,000 km in England and Wales, although recreational facilities are often provided for visitors. The National Trust also owns and protects large areas of coastline. **Long-distance footpaths** often run through conservation areas. These have been established for hikers by the Countryside Commission which gives compensation to local landowners.

Planning Ahead   Planning authorities often find decisions very difficult to make when there are conflicts of interest. They have to balance the needs of the local and national economy with possible damage to the environment caused by litter, pollution and erosion, as well as the cost of any repair work. One way of doing this is to list and weigh up all the economic and social advantages and disadvantages of each development – an **Environmental Impact Analysis**.

1   **a** What is the meaning of the word conservation?
b Describe what has happened to (i) working hours, (ii) holiday time, (iii) car ownership, in recent years.
c Explain why pressure is increasing on the countryside.

2   **a** What are the differences between National Parks and Country Parks?
b Why were National Parks first established?
c Using **C**, draw a pie graph to show land ownership in the Peak District National Park. How does private ownership affect the Park authorities and visitors?
e Suggest why National Park planning boards have a very difficult task in making decisions about new developments in National Parks.

3   Study **D**, then answer the following questions:
a Which activities are related to tourism?
b Which activities are related to local farming, forestry, and industry?
c Which activities involve water resources?
d Which features are related to depopulation (loss of local population)?
e Which one of the following is most likely to represent a conflict of interest, and why?
(i) afforestation and water supply
(ii) beef cattle and sheep farming
(iii) water skiing and reservoirs
(iv) long distance footpaths and farming

D Pressures on the National Parks

Reservoir (water supply to nearby towns and industry)

Long distance footpath

Sheep graze on rough pasture

Beef cattle

Fodder crops

Hay

Moors used for grouse shooting

Mountain hut

Crag used by climbers

Houses for forestry workers

Quarry

Water skiing

Picnic area

Canoeing club

Quarry workers' cottages

Marina

Camping and caravan site

Subaqua

Forestry commission plantation. A planned nature trail passes through part of the forest

Car park

Youth hostel

National Park visitor centre

Village with several 'second homes.' Also popular with retired people

Former village school now used for outdoor activities and adventure courses

37 : The Peak District National Park

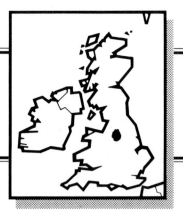

THE PEAK DISTRICT National Park lies mostly in Derbyshire, though it is shared with six other local authorities in the north Midlands (A). It covers 1,400 sq. km of mostly high, open moorland. The population is steady at around 40,000. The only town of any size is Bakewell (population 4,000), but several important roads cross the Park carrying traffic from Derby and Sheffield to Manchester.

Pressures on the Park environment come from many sources:

- **Farming** There are more than 2,300 farms in the Park. Most of them are less than 40 ha and are worked by one farmer and his family. They are mainly dairy or sheep farms. The limestone plateau in the south and the valley floors provide the best grazing. Grouse are reared on many of the moors. Incomes are low, and often made up by second jobs such as quarrying or from providing accommodation for tourists.
- **Water** There are 55 reservoirs over 1½ ha in area within the Park, mostly in the north where impermeable millstone grit is found. They produce 450 million litres of water per day, but there is always the threat of even more valleys being flooded to supply the large urban and industrial centres nearby. Fishing and sailing are allowed on some reservoirs.
- **Extractive Industries** Metals such as lead, copper, zinc and silver were once mined here. Today, 2,000 local people are employed in extraction of minerals. The biggest industry is limestone quarrying. Six million tonnes of limestone are extracted from within the Park every year, and there is continued pressure to expand the quarries. Heavy lorries on steep, narrow roads, air pollution from limestone dust and noise from blasting cause environmental problems.

Limestone and locally-mined shale are used in a large cement works in the Hope Valley. Fluorspar, used in the steel and chemical industries, is obtained from underground mining, opencast excavation and reworking old lead mining spoil heaps. 70% of British fluorspar production comes from within the Park, and demand is increasing. Disposal of toxic waste from the extraction is a growing problem.

Clashes likely over park mining plans

The first of several clashes between conservationists and companies which want to mine in national parks is likely to start at a public enquiry which opens tomorrow.

Tarmac Roadstone Holdings is appealing at Buxton, Derbyshire, against the Peak National Park's refusal to allow the 60-acre Topley Pike quarry, near the town, to be extended by 20 acres.

Topley Pike is an ugly quarry, says the park management, and residents and councils complain about noise and vibration. The nearest hamlet, King Sterndale, is 100 yards away.

Topley produces about 700,000 tonnes of limestone a year and the company says that the extension would safeguard jobs for about 20 years. Tarmac says it is linking the project to long-term restoration of the quarry.

The park, too, sees the quarry being developed for rambling, recreation and nature conservation.

The firm says that the need for the stone is based on its traditional role as supplier to a wide area around Greater Manchester, much of it sent direct by special train. Unions representing some of the 70 workers and self-employed drivers are expected to back the firm's application.

A Tourism in the Peak District National Park

Reservoir
X Campsite
Caravan site
Country park
•••••• Long-distance footpath
Climbing
Caving
T Ancient house or museum
National Park boundary
County boundary
Railway

Glossop
To Manchester
CHESHIRE
Buxton
Bakewell
STAFFORDSHIRE
Ashbourne
SOUTH YORKSHIRE
To Sheffield
Chesterfield
Matlock
DERBYSHIRE
To Nottingham
To Derby

0 5 10 15 20 km

B *Source* The Guardian, April 1985

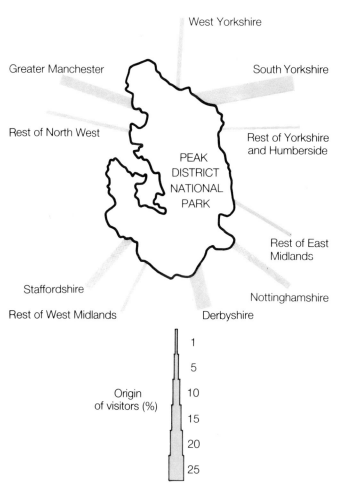

C Day visitors to the Peak District National Park (1986)

West Yorkshire

Greater Manchester

South Yorkshire

Rest of North West

PEAK
DISTRICT
NATIONAL
PARK

Rest of Yorkshire
and Humberside

Rest of East
Midlands

Staffordshire

Nottinghamshire

Rest of West Midlands

Derbyshire

Origin
of visitors (%)

1
5
10
15
20
25

D Path erosion in the Peak District

- **Forestry** The forested area is small. Forestry Commission land is used to grow commercial timber, although the Park Board buys and preserves small mixed woodlands.
- **Settlement** Population is growing in the east of the Park around Bakewell. Many villages here have expanded considerably, but with rising prices, many houses have been occupied by wealthier outsiders. Elsewhere, the population is steady or falling as younger people move away, often in search of jobs. The more remote areas have been hit by a cut in rural bus services.
- **Tourism and Traffic** About 1.5 million people per year stay overnight in the Park while another 17–20 million make day visits. Most of these arrive by private car, and on a fine Sunday, up to 100,000 cars enter the Park. On Easter Monday in 1986, the roads and car parks were so overloaded that police had to turn back day-trippers. Altogether, more than 22 million cars cross the Park boundary annually.

    Apart from the scenery, many tourists are attracted by the large stately homes and by the show caves. Most visitors remain close to the main roads, though many try hiking, caving or climbing. Tourism is one of the main sources of income in the Park. As new car parks and campsites are provided, more visitors are attracted, and the damage to the environment increases, destroying the very features that people come to see.

1 **a** List the features which make the Park attractive to visitors.
b How many day visitors use the Park annually?
c How many visitors stay overnight in the Park each year?
d Which are the main places of origin of the day visitors?
e Would you expect the origins of long-term holidaymakers and day visitors to be similar or different? Give reasons for your answer.
f How do most of the visitors travel to the Park?

2 **a** Copy and complete the diagram below by naming the pressures on the Park.

Peak park

b For each of the pressures you have named, state whether you would (i) ban all future development (ii) tightly restrict all future development, (iii) restrict development in certain areas but allow extensions of existing developments, (iv) allow free expansion in order to meet the demands of the national and local economy. Briefly give the reasons for your choices.

3 Read the extract from the Guardian (**B**). Carry out an Environmental Impact Analysis by listing the advantages and disadvantages of allowing Topley Park quarry to be extended. Make your decision about the extension, then explain it to the conservationists and to the management of Tarmac Roadstone Holdings.

77

38 : Saving The Norfolk Broads

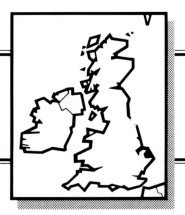

THERE ARE MORE than 40 shallow lakes or broads in the low-lying marshes of eastern Norfolk. The Norfolk Broads were formed by local people digging for peat fuel. When sea level rose during the 14th century, the diggings were flooded. Until this century they remained largely unchanged: fish and wildfowl were a source of food, reeds were cut for thatch and marshes cut for hay. In the twentieth century the Norfolk Broads have developed into a popular holiday area. At the same time, they have come under pressure from farmers keen to drain the marsh and put the fertile soil under intensive arable farming.

A Visitors to Broads
◀ Information Centres, 1986

Total 89,296

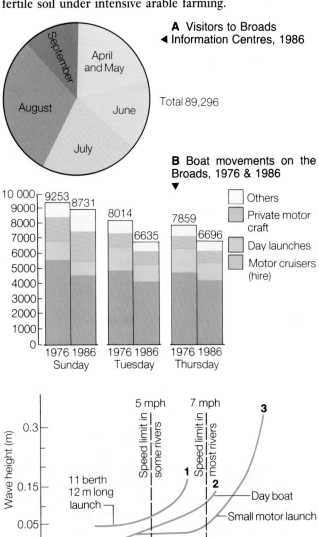

B Boat movements on the Broads, 1976 & 1986 ▼

C Relationship between boat size, speed and wave height

D Aerial view of the Norfolk Broads

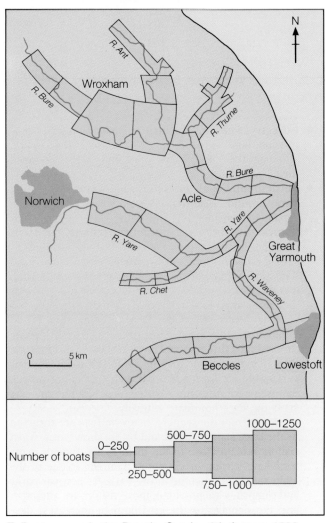

E Boat census in the Broads, Sunday 8th August, 1986

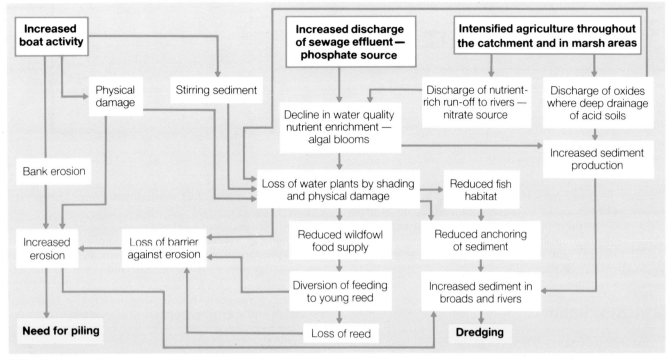

F Environmental impacts on the rivers and the Broads

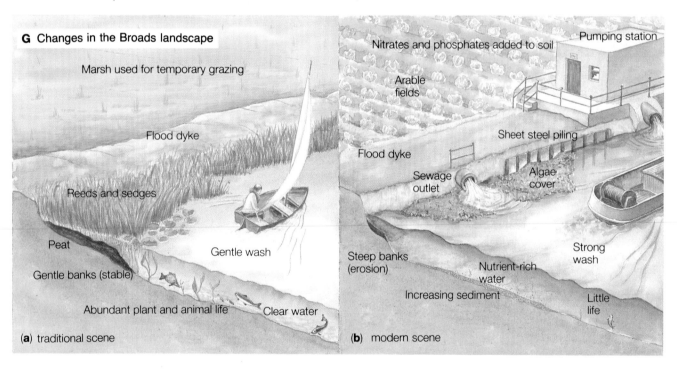

G Changes in the Broads landscape

(a) traditional scene

(b) modern scene

1 Study **A**, **B**, **C** and **E**.
   a Which month is the most popular with visitors to the Broads?
   b Which type of boat is most common on the Broads?
   c What size of boat is most likely to cause rapid wave erosion of the banks?

d Why is 7 mph the speed limit for boats on most rivers?
e Which stretches of river have the most boat traffic?
f What does **B** show about the popularity of boating?
2 Make a list of all the changes which have taken place in the Broads landscape during this century (see **G**).
3 **a** Apart from increased boat activity, what are the two main threats to the environment of the Broads?
   b What are the problems that arise from all these threats to the environment in the Broads (including boating activities)?
   c Taking each problem in turn, suggest a possible solution.

39 : Islands in the Sun

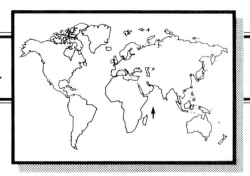

IN RECENT YEARS, longer holidays, more spending power and cheaper air fares have spread tourism to many parts of the world which were once considered remote and inaccessible. Millions of people, especially from Europe and North America, now enjoy holidays on tropical islands or cruising round polar ice caps.

The Seychelles

In the Indian Ocean, 1,600 km from the nearest land, lie the islands of the Seychelles archipelago (**A**). There are more than 100 tiny coral and granite islands spread over 400,000 square kilometres of ocean. The islands were uninhabited until 200 years ago when they were taken over by France. Today's population of mixed European, African and Asian origin speak French, English and a local dialect called Creole.

The islands have warm, sunny weather all year (**C**), white sandy beaches, spectacular mountain scenery, blue waters and coral reefs which support abundant wildlife. There are rare plants and animals such as the coco-de-mer (the largest plant seed in the world) and the giant tortoise.

The population (now 65,000) is growing rapidly: a 50% increase in the last 25 years. The islanders have traditionally been **subsistence** farmers and fishermen, relying on coconuts, cinnamon and vanilla for exports. This way of life began to change when the international airport was opened on Mahé island in 1971. Regular flights replaced the long ocean voyage previously needed to reach the islands.

The Impact of Tourism The government deliberately set out to attract foreign tourists. The first modern hotel was opened in 1972, and today there are a dozen large hotels on Mahé island alone (**B**), together with numerous small hotels, guesthouses and self-catering villas.

About two-thirds of all tourists come from Europe, but visitors from Japan and the Middle East have increased recently. The number of tourists visiting the Seychelles shot up from just over 3,000 in 1971 to a peak of nearly 79,000 in 1979. However, numbers fell sharply in the early 80's as economic recession hit the market and some air services were withdrawn. This led to a 33% loss of income at a time when the government was looking forward to continued expansion and spending more on new facilities.

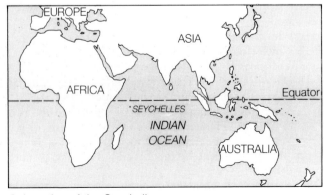

A Location of the Seychelles

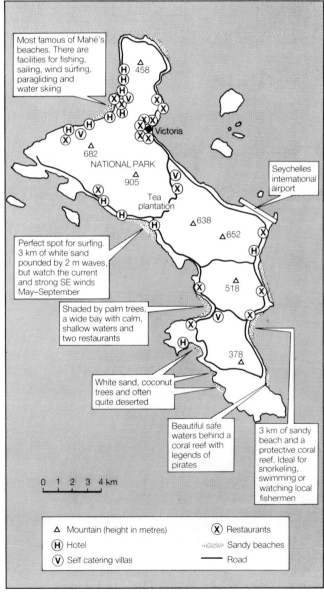

B The island of Mahé in the Seychelles

80

C Holiday facilites in the Seychelles

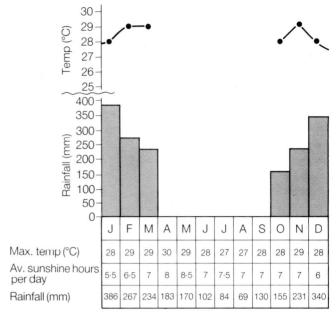

	J	F	M	A	M	J	J	A	S	O	N	D
Max. temp (°C)	28	29	29	30	29	28	27	27	28	28	29	28
Av. sunshine hours per day	5·5	6·5	7	8	8·5	7	7·5	7	7	7	7	6
Rainfall (mm)	386	267	234	183	170	102	84	69	130	155	231	340

D Climate graph and statistics for Victoria, Seychelles

Tourism has become a vital part of the economy of the Seychelles. It accounts for about 35% of government income and provides 70% of foreign exchange earnings. It has taken over as the main source of employment and directly employs 15 – 20% of the work force with at least as many secondary jobs in shops, restaurants and other services. However, when there is a downturn in visitors, jobs are lost, earnings drop, and government income falls.

Considerable efforts are being made to expand the tourist industry. In order to promote domestic tourism, 12 holiday centres are being provided at prices local people can afford. Large sums are being invested in the national airline and in modern hotels, catering and transport.

Other new facilities include exhibition and conference halls, an aquarium, two casinos, a craft centre and development of historical sites and walks. A new training school for people working in tourism has been set up. Plans provide for 100,000 visitors a year by 1988.

1 Imagine you work for the Seychelles tourist board.
a Say where the Seychelles are, as accurately as possible.
b Make a list of the main attractions for visitors.
c Complete the climate graph for Victoria (D).
d Which time of year would you most recommend for a visit? Why?
e Suggest one reason why more Europeans than Africans visit the islands.
2 a Study E. Draw a line graph to show number of visitors 1976–83.
b What variations does your graph show?
c Where do most tourists come from?

d Why was the first modern hotel only built in 1972?
e What are occupancy rates?
f Why did tourist numbers decrease in the early 1980s?
g What problems are caused by an over-reliance on tourism?
3 Study the map of Mahé island (B).
a How large is the island east-west and north-south?
b How far is the capital Victoria from the airport?
c Where are most of the hotels located? Why?
d What dangers occur for swimmers and surfers May-September?
e Are there any threats from tourism to the local environment? If so, what are they?
4 a List the advantages and disadvantages of tourism for the islands.
b Briefly state whether or not you agree with further expansion of the tourist industry. Explain your answer.

Year	Number of visitors	Sources of visitors (%)				Tourist Expenditure (Million R)	Beds Available	Occupancy Rates (%)
		Eur.	Afr.	Asia	Other			
1976	49,498	59.4	26.1	8.6	5.9	—	1870	66
1977	54,490	62.6	23.8	8.0	5.7	195	1970	68
1978	64,995	63.7	21.3	9.2	5.8	243	2170	61
1979	78,852	64.4	17.3	11.7	6.5	291	2430	64
1980	71,762	64.0	16.8	12.2	6.9	326	2560	56
1981	60,425	62.6	15.6	13.4	8.4	285	2680	48
1982	47,280	63.3	15.0	15.3	6.3	220	2690	37
1983	55,867	67.6	14.4	13.6	4.4	233	2770	48

E Tourism in the Seychelles

40 : Extracting Earth's Riches

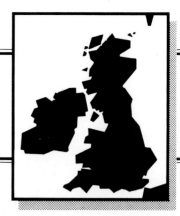

ALL OVER THE WORLD people are digging into the ground to obtain billions of tonnes of raw materials such as fuels, metal ores and building aggregates. This **extractive industry** can only become more widespread as demand for raw materials increases.

Surface Workings

The first raw materials to be exploited are usually at or near the surface. They are most easily discovered and most easily obtained. Rocks such as slate, chalk or limestone are found in large amounts at the surface, so they are obtained cheaply and easily by **quarrying**. Rock is removed by mechanical shovels, diggers and lorries, to leave a huge pit.

Harder rocks such as slate or granite may need to be loosened by blasting before removal, but this is unnecessary for soft rocks such as clay, sand or gravel. In most quarries, the entire rock burden is carried away and no soil or waste remains. This is not the case with china clay (kaolin), a type of decayed granite which is found in Cornwall and Devon. It is washed from the quarry face by high pressure water, then separated from the waste. China clay areas are marked by huge conical waste tips (**B**).

Disused quarries and open pits can leave the countryside scarred by large numbers of man-made ponds and lakes. Many old gravel workings in England are now used for

B Waste tips from Cornwall's china clay quarries

sailing, fishing, and other water sports, or as leisure parks eg Thorpe Park in Surrey.

Metal ores are often low-grade (low in metal content) so that huge amounts of rock have to be mined and processed to obtain relatively small amounts of metal. Waste rock, which is sometimes toxic, is often deposited nearby in man-made lakes. Where large deposits occur at the surface, whole mountain tops may be removed. The largest man-made excavation in the world is a copper mine at Bingham Canyon, Utah, which is 4 km wide and 1 km deep. Such open pits are so large that they will never be filled in or given an alternative use.

Opencast Mining Some minerals such as coal are only found in thin seams (layers). When these seams occur at the surface they are known as **exposed coalfields**. The coal is obtained cheaply by removing the overburden of soil and rock using mechanical excavators, a method known as **opencast mining** (**D**). This can lead to a loss of fertile farmland, but once the seams are exhausted, the waste rock and soil are carefully replaced and the landscape returned to farming or recreation.

Deep Mining

Many minerals have to be obtained from depths of 400 metres or more. This may be because they are scarce at the surface or because the surface deposits have been exhausted. It is then much more difficult and expensive to obtain the minerals, particularly if the seams are interrupted by faults or folds. Sinking shafts and installing equipment is costly and time-consuming. Trapped methane gas can cause explosions.

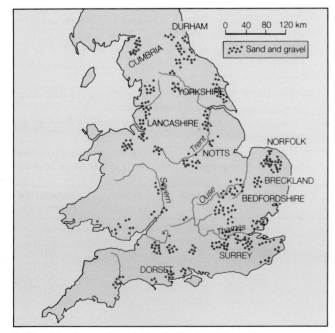

A Sand and gravel workings in England & Wales

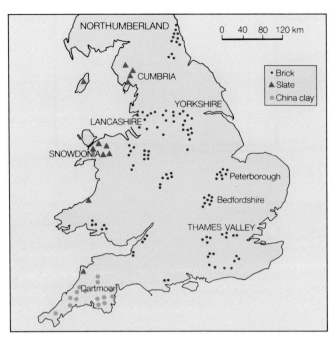

C Location of clay and slate workings in England & Wales

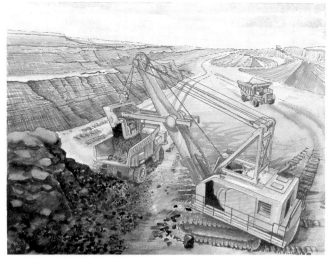

D Northumberland. Butterwell opencast coal mine celebrated its 10th anniversary this year. Operated by Taylor Woodrow Construction Limited for British Coal the site produces in excess of 1 million tonnes annually and is one of the largest opencast sites in Western Europe

Once again, there is a problem of waste disposal. The answer has traditionally been to deposit waste in tips close to the mine. Today, greater efforts are being made to landscape such tips, plant them with vegetation and provide a more pleasant environment.

One other problem associated with extracting materials such as water, oil, salt or coal is **subsidence**. Withdrawal of such materials from underground can cause the surface to sink slowly. The result may be fractured pipes, cracked roads and damaged buildings.

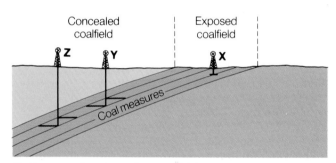

E Cross-section through a coalfield

1 **a** What are extractive industries?
b What is the main difference between quarrying and mining?
c In your own words, write a paragraph explaining the opencast mining method shown in **D**.
2 **a** What is meant by low-grade ore?
b Why are there no waste tips near sand, chalk or limestone quarries?
c Why are there often waste tips near china clay workings, metal ore mines and coal mines?
d What is meant by subsidence?
e Why is subsidence often linked with extractive industries?
3 **a** Study **F**. Which two non-fuel minerals are most important in Britain?
b How many million tonnes of non-fuel minerals are obtained each year in Britain?
c What is the main use of these non-fuel minerals?
d Describe the distribution of sand and gravel workings in England and Wales (see **A**).
e Which industry would you expect to find in Bedfordshire and near Peterborough? Why?

4 **a** Study **E**. What is the difference between an exposed coalfield and a concealed coalfield?
b Which mine (X, Y or Z) would you expect to be the oldest? Why?
c Which mine (X, Y or Z) would you expect to be most expensive to open and operate? Why?
d Which mine would you expect to close first? Why?
e Which mine (X, Y or Z) is most likely to be opencast? Why?

Mineral	Output (1984) m. tonnes	Main uses
Sand & gravel	106	Building eg concrete
Coal	104.5	Fuel, electricity, iron & steel
Limestone	93.5	Lime, iron & steel, cement
Igneous rock eg granite	36.8	Building, roads
Clay & shale	17.8	Bricks, pottery, tiles
Sandstone	15.1	Building
Chalk	12.0	Lime, cement
Salt	7.1	Chemicals, domestic salt
China clay	3.6	Pottery, paper, toothpaste, polish
Gypsum	3.1	Plaster of Paris, plasterboard, food
Potash	0.5	Fertiliser, chemicals
Iron ore	0.4	Iron & steel

F Some common British minerals

41 : Oil in Alaska

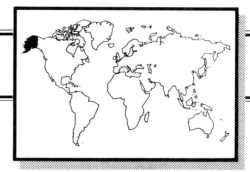

WITHOUT OIL, there would be few plastics, man-made fibres or chemicals, and transport would grind to a halt. Experts suggest that known oil reserves will run out in 60 years, so the search is on for new reserves in the last unexplored sites – the polar regions and sea floor.

Alaska is part of the United States of America. About one third of it lies within the Arctic Circle, but the south coast is ice-free, and this is where most of the people live. In the early 1960's, about 250,000 people lived in Alaska, over one fifth of them in the town of Anchorage. The state was described as the last great wilderness in North America.

On 27 March 1964, the south coast was struck by one of the most powerful earthquakes on record. Property damage in Anchorage alone was estimated at $285 million. The final death toll was put at 115. Then, in 1968, there was a major oil strike at Prudhoe Bay on the North Slope beside the Arctic Ocean. The development of this oilfield was essential to the United States, since it would reduce dependence on imported foreign oil. But how could the oil be transported to the markets in mainland USA firstly, without being threatened by future possible earthquakes, and secondly without damaging the fragile environment?

Tundra Winter lasts for 9–10 months in the tundra region of northern Alaska. With sub-zero temperatures, the ground freezes hard. This **permafrost** remains solid all year except for perhaps the top metre which briefly thaws. In summer this top layer can become unstable and shift downhill when it becomes saturated, then heave upwards when it freezes.

In such conditions, meltwater cannot easily drain away or evaporate, so large areas remain bog. Scars on the landscape take a long time to disappear, bacteria and plants are only active for a short time. Only lichens and quick-flowering plants can survive. There are no trees. Herds of caribou, wild cousins of the reindeer, survive by migrating long distances each summer in search of grazing land.

The Pipeline

The oil companies finally decided to build a pipeline and service road 1270 km across Alaska from Prudhoe Bay to the port of Valdez (**A**). This meant bringing in more than 20,000 workers for the four year job. It also meant crossing three mountain ranges, more than 800 streams, and 950 km of permafrost as well as the annual caribou migration routes.

Great efforts were made to cause the minimum ecological damage. For more than half its length, the pipe is lifted about four metres above ground level (**B**). It rests on 78,000 vertical supports filled with heat-absorbing slurry (sand and

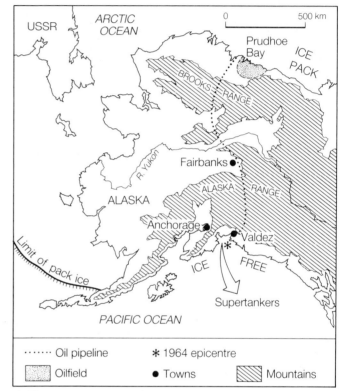

A The 1964 Alaskan earthquake and the recent oil developments

water) and liquid ammonia to prevent the warm pipe from melting the permafrost. The pipe itself is insulated, both to keep the oil warm and easy to pump, and to ensure that the permafrost remains frozen. Where it crosses caribou migration routes or streams, the pipe is buried. Small pipes filled with liquid brine keep the permafrost solid in areas of instability (**C**).

Concrete jackets surround the pipe beneath streams, though 13 rivers are crossed by bridge, including the 750 metre span over the Yukon River. Pumping stations are located where they do not interfere with wildlife, and new vegetation has often been planted over bare scars.

Other precautions include flexible pipe which can bend in an earthquake, and regularly spaced valves designed to close automatically if a break occurs. The town and oil storage installations at Valdez were moved to a new site on bedrock above tsunami level after the 1964 earthquake. Nevertheless, about 300 oil spills of more than 375 litres (100 gallons) were recorded along the pipeline between 1970 and 1986. The service road has also opened up the interior to hunters and tourists. Conservationists strongly oppose any new oil developments in Alaska.

B The Alaskan oil pipeline

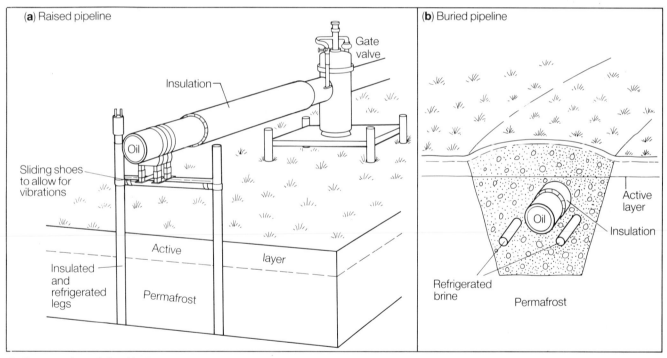

C Construction of the Alaska oil pipeline

1 **a** Where was the oil strike in Alaska in 1968?
b How far is the oilfield from Valdez?
c Why did a pipeline have to be built to Valdez?
d Why did port installations at Valdez have to be moved?
e Why were the oil companies prepared to spend millions of pounds on the pipeline?

2 **a** What is permafrost?
b Make a list of the construction problems which faced the people building the pipeline.
c Why were conservationists worried about the pipeline project?
d For each problem you have listed in **b** and **c**, explain how the oil companies tried to overcome them.

3 Several more oil and gas pipelines are projected for tundra regions in future. Carry out an Environmental Impact Analysis by listing all of the advantages and disadvantages of such schemes. After weighing them up, make a final decision in favour or against.

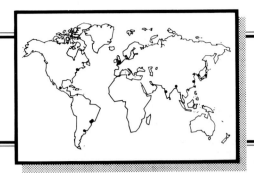

42 : The Urban Explosion

THE WORLD'S PEOPLE are increasingly becoming town and city dwellers. In the year 1800, only about one in forty (2½%) of the world population lived in settlements of more than 20,000 inhabitants. By 1970 this figure had risen to about one in four (25%), and it is expected to rise to one in two (50%) by the end of this century.

World Trends   The urban population explosion is not the same in all countries. The rural populations of western Europe and North America began to drift to the towns during the Industrial Revolution. Over the last 200 years, people in these countries have come to rely on urban centres for jobs, services, housing and transport. Supplies of water, power and food are ensured by efficient service systems and modern mechanised agriculture. As a result, countries such as the UK and USA will have more than 80% of their people living in urban areas by the year 2000.

In developing countries, **subsistence** agriculture keeps nearly all of the people tied to the land. People in these countries have only recently begun to leave the farms and villages as industries have grown up in the towns and cities.

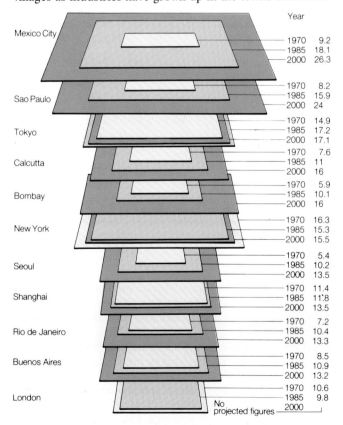

	Year	
Mexico City	1970	9.2
	1985	18.1
	2000	26.3
Sao Paulo	1970	8.2
	1985	15.9
	2000	24
Tokyo	1970	14.9
	1985	17.2
	2000	17.1
Calcutta	1970	7.6
	1985	11
	2000	16
Bombay	1970	5.9
	1985	10.1
	2000	16
New York	1970	16.3
	1985	15.3
	2000	15.5
Seoul	1970	5.4
	1985	10.2
	2000	13.5
Shanghai	1970	11.4
	1985	11.8
	2000	13.5
Rio de Janeiro	1970	7.2
	1985	10.4
	2000	13.3
Buenos Aires	1970	8.5
	1985	10.9
	2000	13.2
London	1970	10.6
	1985	9.8
	No projected figures 2000	

A Comparison between growth rates of different cities

B Shanty town and modern flats, Bombay

If this trend continues, cities in the developing world will have an overall increase of 1.3 billion people by the year 2000. There are already some 60 cities with more than 1 million people (**C**): by the end of the century there will be nearly 300 of them. At least 20 cities will have populations of more than 20 million.

The Urban Magnet

More than half of the urban growth in developing countries is due to a combination of high birth rates and reduced death rates which cause a natural increase of 2–3% a year. However, cities are also expanding because of a **push-pull process**.

Rapidly rising population means it is harder to earn a living from small farms, especially if farms are divided between families when their owners die. Introduction of machines and modern farming methods means fewer

Continent	Number of cities over 1 million	
	in 1960	in 1980
N. America	7	14
S. America	3	6
Africa	2	8
Europe	6	8
Asia	8	19
Australasia	1	5

C Number of cities over 1 million people

workers are needed. Many farmers do not own their land and can be evicted by their landlords. High rural unemployment and poverty **push** people from the land to nearby towns and then to cities. People are **pulled** into cities looking for jobs and a better standard of living. Average earnings are two to ten times higher in the cities.

Meeting People's Needs   The cities cannot cope with an influx of up to 1,000 people each day. Houses and jobs cannot be created fast enough to meet demand. The newcomers build their own shacks from pieces of wood or metal sheeting on any waste land they can find (**B**). These **shanty towns** have open drains, no paved roads, no gas or electricity, and no clean piped water. The transport system is also unable to cope. The lucky ones find jobs and are able to move into new houses, but millions of people face malnutrition, disease, unemployment and poverty (**D**).

In the face of these problems, city authorities struggle to build cheap houses, provide basic sanitation and services, and create more jobs. Unfortunately, many poor countries are already heavily in debt to foreign banks, so the money for such schemes is hard to obtain. One expert calculated that $7 billion per year of foreign aid is needed to overcome the problems of city slums in developing countries.

50m slum-dwellers to face orders to move

By BALRAM TANDON in New Delhi

The venerable judges of India's Supreme Court recently handed down a judgment which virtually sounds the death knell for an estimated 50 million people who live in slums built without authorisation on Government land.

In Bombay alone half of the city's nine million population face the grim prospect of losing their homes when the local administration decides to start a clean-up.

Calcutta is said to have even more slums than Bombay and these teem with people living in the most appalling conditions, without electricity, ventilation, drainage or public conveniences.

Sewer pipes

In all three major cities millions of people are born, grow up and die in huts built by railway lines, on pavements, under bridges and sometimes in the huge ferro-concrete tubes awaiting the laying of a sewer system.

Thousands have less than one square metre of space under a small canvas strip. Some of these families, the poorest of poor ragpickers, actually pay rent for their hovels to extortionist "pavement landlords".

The judges noted the squalor of the pavement dwellers' lives: "They cook and sleep where they please, for no conveniences are available to them".

But a recent study in Bombay showed that 50 per cent of the families had incomes of less than 500 rupees (about £30) a month and 32 per cent had 1,000 rupees a month.

The problem of the major cities is simple: 35 years after independence they are big magnets for the unemployed or semi-employed. Bombay and Calcutta continue to be cities of adventure for the young seeking to make quick fortunes.

Many of the slum dwellers say that they would gladly move provided they were given alternative accommodation.

Fig. D The problem of shanty towns in India

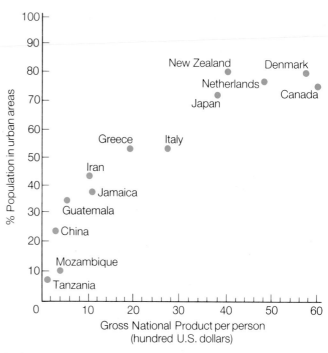

E Scattergram showing relationship between gross national product (GNP) and urban population in selected countries

1 **a** What percentage of the world's people lived in urban areas in 1800 and 1970?
   b What percentage of the world's people will live in urban areas in the year 2000?
   c What does **C** tell you about modern urban growth?
   d Gross National Product (GNP) is a measure of a country's wealth. What does **E** show you about present urbanisation?
   e On an outline map of the world, mark and name the world's largest cities listed in **A**.
   f Name two large cities which are still growing rapidly, and two which are no longer growing rapidly.
   g Briefly suggest why the cities named in **f** are growing at different rates.
2 Name four push and four pull pull factors which cause people to move to cities from the countryside.
3 **a** What is a shanty town?
   b Describe the likely conditions in a shanty town.
   c Why is improvement very difficult in developing cities?
   d If you were mayor of a rapidly expanding city in a developing country, explain how you would try to improve conditions in shanty towns.

43 : Green Belts and New Towns

DURING THIS CENTURY, the population of Great Britain has increased from 32.5 million to 56.3 million. This means there is now less space available to support each person in the country, although there are regional variations.

For most of the century, urban areas have attracted large numbers of people while rural populations have been declining (A). More recently, people have begun to leave the decaying inner cities to live in the suburbs or smaller country towns. Prosperous south-east England has been the main magnet for migration from areas of high unemployment such as the north-east and Merseyside.

The Green Belts

By the 1950's there was a danger that a continuous built-up area might soon extend from London through the Midlands to northern England. Britain's cities had rapidly spread outwards, swallowing up nearby towns and villages to form giant **conurbations**. Urban growth had to be controlled.

New planning laws in the 1950's set out to control this growth by establishing green belts around major cities. The first was the London green belt (**B**). In the green belts, new housing and industrial development are restricted in favour of agriculture, woodland and leisure. Today, there are 15 green belts covering nearly 12% of England and Wales. They vary greatly in size from 485,000 ha around London to less than 1,000 ha around Burton-on-Trent.

Green belts are always under pressure from developers. This is especially true today when demand for housing around London is high. An estimated 460,000 new houses will be required in the south-east by 2001. Plans have been put forward for new towns, industrial estates and giant shopping centres close to the new M25 motorway (**E**).

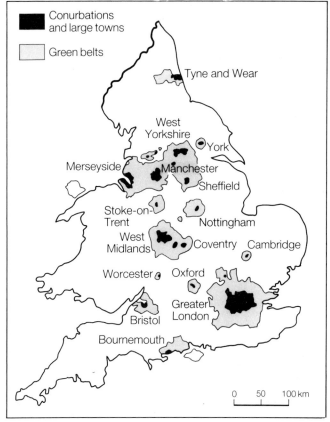

B Green belts in England & Wales

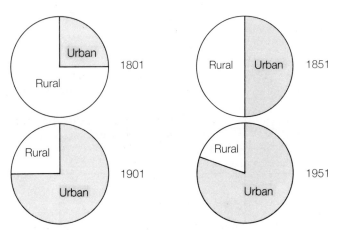

A The changing urban-rural balance of UK population

C Farmland disappearing under houses

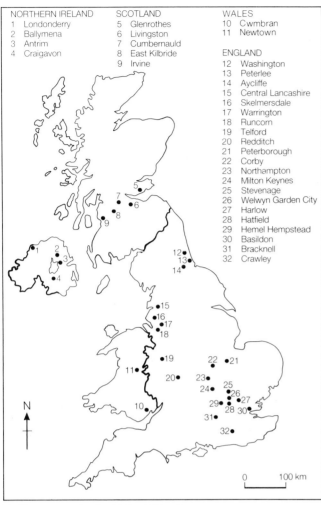

NORTHERN IRELAND	SCOTLAND	WALES
1 Londonderry	5 Glenrothes	10 Cwmbran
2 Ballymena	6 Livingston	11 Newtown
3 Antrim	7 Cumbernauld	
4 Craigavon	8 East Kilbride	ENGLAND
	9 Irvine	12 Washington
		13 Peterlee
		14 Aycliffe
		15 Central Lancashire
		16 Skelmersdale
		17 Warrington
		18 Runcorn
		19 Telford
		20 Redditch
		21 Peterborough
		22 Corby
		23 Northampton
		24 Milton Keynes
		25 Stevenage
		26 Welwyn Garden City
		27 Harlow
		28 Hatfield
		29 Hemel Hempstead
		30 Basildon
		31 Bracknell
		32 Crawley

D New towns in the United Kingdom

New Towns

Another way of controlling urban growth has been to build new planned settlements. The first examples of these were the 'garden cities' of Letchworth and Welwyn Garden City which were built in the early twentieth century.

Since the New Towns Act of 1946, this idea has been developed with the creation of new and expanded towns. People from crowded inner cities are offered modern houses and jobs in a planned urban environment. Industry is attracted by new premises with good communications and cheap land. Today there are 33 new towns in the UK (**D**), mostly located near the conurbations or in areas of high unemployment. When they are completed, these new towns are expected to house more than 3.5 million people.

In addition, there are 28 expanded towns, mostly in the Midlands and East Anglia. These are established towns which have agreed to take people in order to stimulate their own economic development and to help reduce overcrowding and congestion in London and other conurbations.

Development headaches as M25 is finished

By John Grigsby
Local Government
Correspondent

MORE THAN 40 years after it was first proposed, developers, politicians and planners have begun to tackle the opportunities and problems posed by the M25, the world's longest city by-pass.

The final eight-mile section between Bricket Wood and South Mimms opens on Wednesday, marking the beginning of a major headache for everyone involved in protecting the Green Belt and guiding developement in the South East.

Almost every week over the last year, proposals for new developments have been announced along or near the 117 mile, £1,000 million road.

At the last count, there were proposals for at least seven motorway service areas, nine out-of-town shopping centres, nine large "new villages", as well as three "high-tech" industrial parks.

The road's completion conjures up the vision of a new kind of city in which executives seldom venture into the centre but commute round the motorway between country towns like St Albans and Chertsey, or Redhill and Waltham Cross.

Mr Richard Bate, senior planner with the Council for the Protection of Rural England, said yesterday: "The final link will now mean that developers will really be able to get going with their schemes.

"It is going to put great pressures on to the countryside, particularly in Hertfordshire and Kent."

Already a public inquiry is being held into plans to build a service station at Titsey Wood, between Westerham in Kent and Oxted, Surrey.

Conservationists believe the services would threaten an area of outstanding natural beauty and become a magnet for further developments.

The Government has answered the fears of local councils and of Conservative MPs in the South East by insisting that there should be no ribbon development along the motorway.

E The M25 and Green Belt development

1 a Describe what **A** shows about changes in the urban-rural balance of UK population.
b Study **F**. How much farmland has been lost through urbanisation 1922–1980?
c Draw a bar graph to show losses of farmland due to urbanisation in England and Wales 1922–1980.
d In which five-year period was the loss of farmland for building greatest?
e Why is London an example of a conurbation?
2 a How many new towns are there in the UK?
b Where are most of these new towns located?
c Why have the new towns been built?
3 a What is an urban green belt ?
b What types of land use are restricted in green belts, and what types of land use are allowed or encouraged?
4 Study **E**.
a How and why has the M25 motorway increased the threat to London's green belt?
b Do you think new developments such as those mentioned in the article should be allowed? Give reasons for your answer.
c Which of these solutions to the housing problem would you favour? Explain your choice.
● abolish green belt,
● allow housing along main routes,
● limit new development to derelict land.

F Loss of farmland in England & Wales due to urbanisation 1922–80 (Area in thousands of hectares)

Years	1922–26	1927–31	1932–36	1937–39	1940–45	1946–50	1951–55	1956–60	1960–65	1966–70	1971–75	1976–80
Area	9.1	21.1	25.1	25.1	5.3	17.5	15.5	14.0	15.3	16.8	14.9	9.3

44 : Britain's Wasted Land

LAND WHICH HAS been badly damaged by industrial and other development so that it cannot be used without treatment is known as **derelict** land. Large sums of money are needed to bring such land back into use. Over 70,000 ha of Britain are lying derelict, and the area is gradually increasing, despite efforts at restoration.

Derelict land comes in many forms. One of the most widespread is waste tips from mines and quarries. Cornwall suffers most from this because of its old tin and copper mines, and china clay workings. Old clay or gravel pits and quarries are often too large to fill in. These pits often become flooded, creating a landscape of man-made ponds.

Old mine buildings and factories may be left standing long after the industry has closed down. This has been most noticeable in northern England, South Wales and central Scotland, where coalmining and heavy industries such as iron and steel or shipbuilding have declined in recent years. Decaying industrial sites account for nearly 50% of derelict land in the north west, the region with the most overall dereliction in Britain (**A** and **C**). In addition, more than 8,000 ha of derelict railway land have been left through closure of uneconomic lines since the 1960's.

One of the major areas of dereliction today is in the inner cities. These inner city areas were the home of thriving industries and terraced houses in the 19th century. Today, the industries have largely closed down, moved to new sites on the edge of the city or moved to new towns. Often the workers have moved with them.

Redevelopment or Renovation?

Derelict land can be brought back into use – at a cost. With the help of government grants and urban development corporations, local authorities and industry have created some impressive new developments.

B Derelict land in the inner city

In rural areas, waste land can be restored to agriculture after landscaping and use of fertilisers. Old gravel pits are suitable for water sports eg the Holme Pierrepont National Water Sport Centre.

In urban or industrial areas, old tips, railway yards and industrial sites can be turned into parks for recreation and tourism. The Liverpool International Garden Festival was built partly on a disused oil tank farm and partly on a refuse disposal site. Valuable sites near main roads may be returned to housing, shopping and modern industrial estates. The Gateshead Metrocentre is a privately-built shopping complex on the site of a disused power station.

Region	Spoil heaps	Excavation and pits	Military etc. dereliction	Derelict railway land	Other forms eg industry, housing	Total
North	1872	1043	168	1375	2849	7307
North West	2012	1318	398	1648	4603	10042
Yorkshire & Humberside	1070	1433	385	1428	1115	5431
West Midlands	2174	917	330	875	1491	5787
East Midlands	1225	1258	644	1339	732	5198
East Anglia	15	305	251	170	63	804
South West	4870	420	208	820	317	6635
South East (ex G.L.)	57	1439	268	374	387	2525
Greater London	45	382	364	181	982	1954
Total for England	13340	8578	3016	8210	12539	45683

A Types of derelict land by region in England, 1982 (ha)

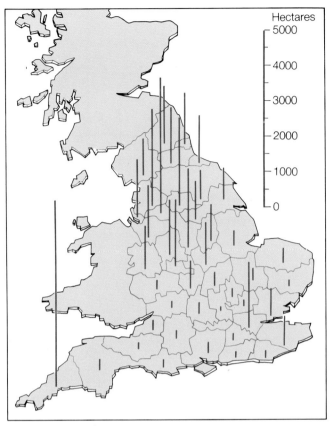

C Distribution of derelict land in English counties, 1982

Large **redevelopment** schemes in many cities during the 1960's and 1970's led to demolition of old houses. Residents were housed in concrete tower blocks built on the sites of their old terraces, moved to new estates on the outskirts of the city, or moved to new towns. Tower blocks are not popular with residents and have often been found to be damp and unsafe. Councils now favour **renovation** (modernisation) of old houses to keep communities together in inner city areas. More recently, private housing has been encouraged in the inner cities, especially in Enterprise Zones which attract new jobs eg the London docklands.

1 **a** What is meant by derelict land?
b Make a list of the main types of derelict land. Put them in order of importance.
c What does **A** tell you about the distribution of derelict land in England?
d Why is there so much derelict land in Cornwall?
e Why is there so much derelict land in NW England?
f What makes up the 'other forms of dereliction' in Greater London?
g What is the difference between urban redevelopment and renovation?
2 **a** Explain why the problem of derelict land is difficult to solve.
b If you were Minister of the Environment, how would you attempt to solve the problem?

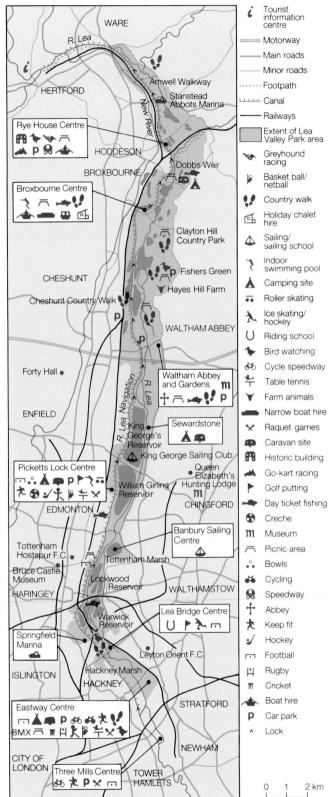

D Lee Valley Country Park (1986)

3 The Lee Valley in north east London was once described as 'a wilderness of gravel pits, factories, derelict buildings and sewage works'. Study **D**.
a How large is the Lee Valley Country Park?
b List the various activities found in the Park under these headings: Leisure. Historical Heritage. Agriculture. Access.

91

45 : Docklands Without Ships

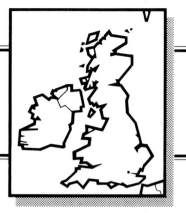

LONDON'S OLD DOCKLANDS stretch 10km down-stream from Tower Bridge along both banks of the River Thames.

Soft London Clay was easy to excavate, even in Victorian times. The oldest and smallest docks were built upstream near the City. These were the first to close in 1967. Meanwhile, as ships became larger and cargoes were containerised, new docks were built downstream. There the river was wider and deeper, there was more room for expansion, and new loading facilities could be provided.

Derelict Dockland By 1981, all the old docks of London had been closed to commercial traffic. As the docks closed, the traditional jobs disappeared. The number of dockers fell from 18,000 to fewer than 3,000. Local councils in Dockland formed a joint committee to build new houses and create new jobs, but without much success.

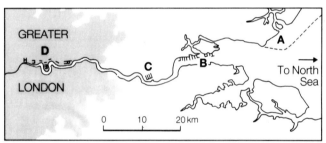

A Location of London docks

The Docklands Development Corporation

In 1981, the government set up the Docklands Development Corporation whose job was to attract private investment to the area. A special Enterprise Zone was created in the heart of Docklands (**B**). Firms moving there are freed from any rates and taxes until 1992, and planning procedures are easier.

The government is investing over £200 million to create modern services, communications and transport. A major selling point is the closeness to the City, only 10–20 minutes' travel from the docks. Improvements to transport include new bus services, a new light railway, a proposed river launch service and a STOL (short take-off and landing) airport.

All of this has attracted a variety of enterprises. These include newspaper printing plants, Billingsgate fish market, Limehouse TV studios, Mercury telecommunications and the National Indoor Sports Centre.

The largest development of all is the £2 billion Canary Wharf proposal (**C**). It is intended to act as a new computerised financial centre outside the overcrowded City. The scheme involves building three giant tower blocks together with other blocks, open spaces, shops and restaurants. It will be so big that it will need its own telephone, electricity, water and rail systems. 57,000 permanent new jobs will be created.

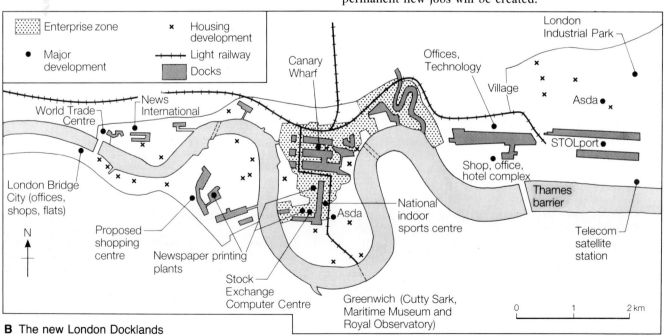

B The new London Docklands

The population of Docklands is expected to increase from 40,000 to 65,000 between 1981 and 1990. Luxury flats and houses are springing up all over Docklands (**C**), but especially along the riverfront where old warehouses are being redeveloped. 6,500 houses were built between 1981 and 1986, but rising demand means prices are doubling each year.

The Objectors The Dockland developments are not popular with everyone. Local people complain of rich executives moving into expensive flats while there is a shortage of cheap housing. Booming house prices and lack of suitable jobs are forcing older residents to leave the area. High technology firms employ only a few people with special skills, so local people do not benefit. They believe that existing jobs should be protected and more public housing provided.

1 **a** Give two advantages of the location of the old docks.
b Which docks closed first?
c Why did the older docks lose their trade?
d Copy A. Add a key naming
● the oldest docks, ● the newer docks enlarged in 1960s, ● the jetties for large oil tankers, ● possible site of future docks.
e Give reasons for your choices in **d**.

2 **a** Why was the Docklands Development Corporation set up in 1981?
b What is the Docklands Enterprise Zone?
c Name three different new developments in the Enterprise Zone.
d What are the main attractions for new businesses in Docklands?
e Why are house or flat prices very high and doubling every year?
f Describe and explain the changes which will occur as a result of the new Canary Wharf development.
g What objections might people have to development of Canary Wharf?

3 **a** Look at the diagram on the left. Write down the arguments you think the businessman and the local resident would make for and against the way docklands are being developed.
b With which person do you agree? Why?

C Canary Wharf. The biggest property development in the world.

46 : Pollution

THE WORD POLLUTION can be defined as:

> The introduction into the environment, by people, of substances or energy liable to cause harm to living creatures or ecological systems.

Four main areas of pollution can be recognised: air pollution, water pollution, land pollution and noise pollution. In each case, the environment is affected by the introduction of substances or energy not normally found in nature.

Some of these pollutants, such as smoke, are easily seen and recognised. Measures can be taken to reduce their effects, and the success or failure of these measures can be seen by everyone. Other substances, such as carbon dioxide in the air or nitrates in water, are invisible and can only be detected by sensitive scientific instruments. The effects of such chemicals are often not immediately obvious.

There is much debate over the cost and the need to reduce pollution. Governments or companies may not want to spend large sums of money which will put up taxes or prices, or reduce profits, unless the benefits to everyone are obvious. As a result, numerous pressure groups have grown up to monitor pollution and to persuade MPs or companies to improve the environment.

Air Pollution Earth's atmosphere contains about 77% nitrogen and 21% oxygen. The remaining 2% is made up of many other gases. Some of these are added to the atmosphere by volcanic eruptions, by vegetation or by bacterial decay. However, particularly since the beginning of the Industrial Revolution some 200 years ago, more and more man-made pollutants have been pumped into the atmosphere eg carbon dioxide, smoke, lead, and sulphur. These are carried long distances by the wind and affect regions far from the pollution source (see unit 49).

Land Pollution This is mainly due to the disposal of liquid and solid wastes. In the past, most rubbish was bio-degradable – it would decay naturally, eventually being completely consumed by the action of insects, fungi and bacteria, and returned to the soil as humus.

Today, more rubbish is generated than ever before and new synthetic substances such as plastics are not bio-degradable. Recycling is either not possible or too expensive, so every year 2 billion tonnes of waste are buried in the EEC alone. Much of this is placed in old quarries or mines, though some is used for land reclamation. Disposal of toxic wastes from chemical works and radioactive waste from nuclear facilities is also a matter of major concern.

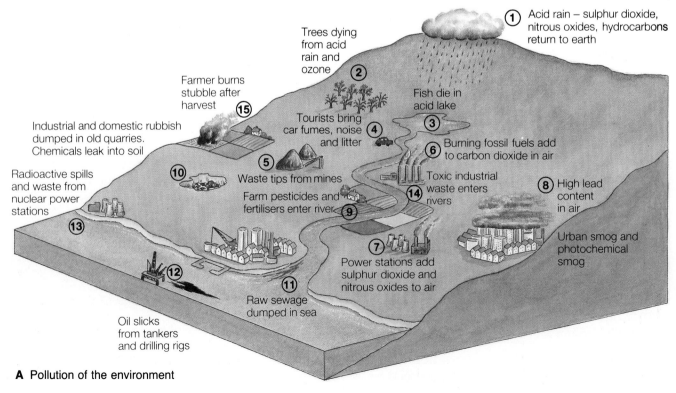

A Pollution of the environment

B Burning an oil slick

Water Pollution Natural water supplies are not always pure, but many inland and coastal waters which were once clean have been contaminated by pollution. Over half the rivers in the United States have been officially designated as polluted – unfit for drinking or recreation.

Some pollution is caused by accidental spillages, as with oil tankers running aground (**B** and **C**) or fires in chemical works located beside rivers. Other pollution involves careless disposal of waste and sewage. A 1975 US government survey showed that two-thirds of all industries discharged wastes directly into rivers. The total clean-up bill was estimated as $600 billion (about £340,000,000!).

Noise Pollution The introduction of machines has made modern life much noisier than ever before (**E**). Actual physical damage to the environment is slight, though sonic booms from supersonic aircraft can damage buildings. More important is the decline in the quality of life for the people affected, particularly near airports and busy roads.

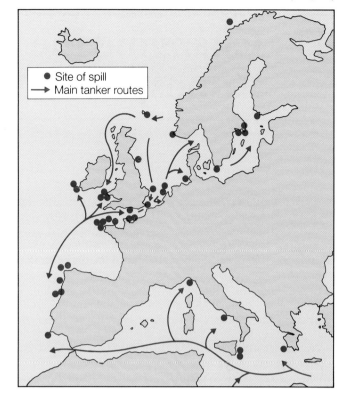

Fig. C Tanker spills over 700 tonnes 1970–1980

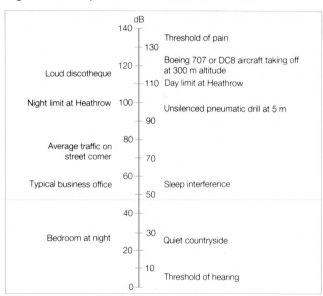

E Typical noise levels in dB (decibels)

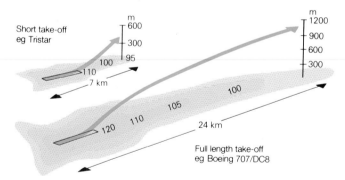

D Noise footprints during take-off measured in decibels

1 **a** What is pollution?
b Why has it become a more serious problem in the last 200 years?
2 With the help of **A**, make a list of any pollutants you have come across or know about. An example is given to help you. Use these headings:

Pollution Type	Pollutant	Source
Air	Lead	Car exhausts

3 **a** Study **C**. How many large oil tanker spillages took place in European waters during the 1970's?
b Where were most of these spillages?
c Explain your answer to **b**.
4 Study **D** and **E**.
a What dB (decibel) level would most people have experienced 200 years ago?
b What range of decibel levels do you usually experience each day?
c How would a STOL (short take-off and landing) aircraft help solve the noise problem?
d Why is double glazing not an ideal solution to excess noise?

47 : Changing the Atmosphere

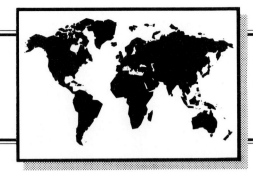

CARBON DIOXIDE is not present in very large amounts in Earth's atmosphere (about 0.03% by volume). However, it is a very important gas because plants need it to grow through the process of photosynthesis. Without carbon dioxide there would be no plant or animal life on Earth (**E**).

The Greenhouse Effect   Until the Industrial Revolution and the world population explosion, the amount of carbon dioxide in the atmosphere seems to have stayed about the same. During the last 200 years the balance in the carbon cycle has changed, partly because forests have been cut down, but mainly because carbon dioxide is emitted when wood and **fossil fuels** such as coal, oil and natural gas are burnt (**C** and **D**). Perhaps half of this extra carbon dioxide is dissolved in the oceans, leaving the remainder to build up in the atmosphere.

Short wave solar radiation is able to pass through the atmosphere and heat Earth's surface. However, when the warm surface radiates the heat back into the atmosphere, it is at a longer (infra-red) wavelength than the incoming solar radiation. Carbon dioxide (and a few other rare gases such as methane and ammonia) act like a sheet of glass in a greenhouse and reflect back the infra-red radiation – this is called the **greenhouse effect** (**A**). The heat trapped in the atmosphere will raise the temperature of the atmosphere.

The Problem   Estimates suggest that the level of carbon dioxide in the atmosphere will double over the next 100 years, resulting in a rise of mean global temperature of perhaps 2–3°C. No-one knows exactly what the effects of an increase in carbon dioxide will be.

Different climates might be affected in different ways:
- The world's wind and pressure belts would change, causing the climates to change. For example, the westerly winds would blow less frequently over Britain, causing warmer, drier summers and colder winters.
- The temperature rise would be greater in the northern hemisphere where there is a larger land surface.
- Higher latitudes would be warmed more than lower latitudes. This has led to a fear that the polar ice sheets would begin to melt, raising sea level and flooding low-lying coastal areas.
- The tropics would generally become wetter.
- The dry desert regions would become even more arid and tend to spread, leading to even greater poverty and starvation than today.

If the temperate grasslands of Europe and North America become drier, the main food surplus regions could turn into dust bowls with a disastrous decline in crop yields and a world food shortage. On the other hand, while yields of cereals and potatoes might fall, other plants such as sugar beet, grass and coniferous forests would yield more.

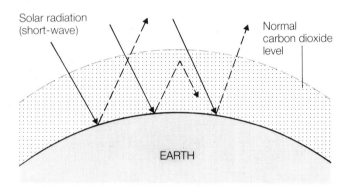

(a)   Some long-wave infra-red radiation (heat) is reflected and absorbed by carbon dioxide. Some heat escapes into space

Solar radiation (short-wave)

Normal carbon dioxide level

EARTH

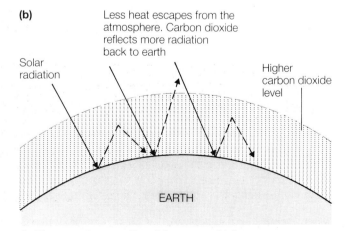

(b)   Less heat escapes from the atmosphere. Carbon dioxide reflects more radiation back to earth

Solar radiation

Higher carbon dioxide level

EARTH

A The greenhouse effect (a) present (b) future

USA 223

USSR 233

Western Europe 127

Rest of world 123

China 99

79 Eastern Europe

B World coal reserves (thousand million tonnes)

96

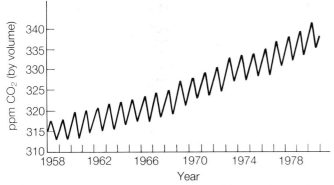

C Monthly average concentrations of CO_2 at Mauna Loa Observatory, Hawaii. (Peaks and troughs due to variations between summer and winter)

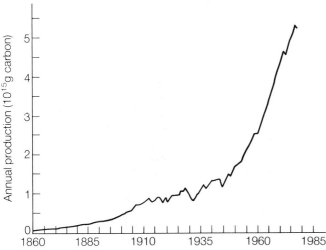

D Annual world carbon dioxide production from fossil fuel combustion and cement manufacture

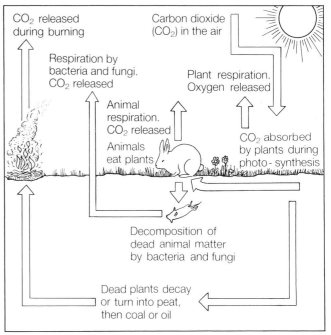

E The carbon cycle

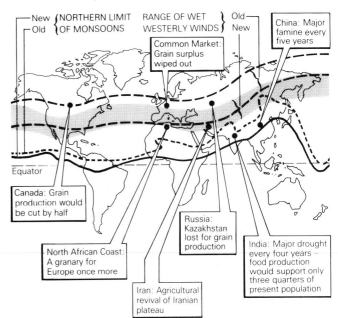

F Consequences of a little ice age

The Answer The only solution is to cut back on burning fossil fuels. At present, most of the carbon dioxide is emitted through burning coal. Unless this changes, perhaps through increased use of nuclear power or the introduction of renewable energy sources such as wind or water, it is difficult to see how the carbon dioxide emissions can be reduced. World coal reserves could last for another 200 years or more, so coal will probably remain very important in a world short of energy. However, there is also a theory that pollutants in the upper atmosphere may block out sunlight and cause a 'little ice age' in the near future (**F**).

1   **a** Why are the changes caused by increased carbon dioxide called the greenhouse effect?
  b Explain how the greenhouse effect operates.
  c What is the link between carbon dioxide and plant growth?
  d What would happen to the carbon dioxide level if large areas of the world were deforested? Explain your answer.

2   **a** What are fossil fuels?
  b What was the mean volume of carbon dioxide in the atmosphere in (i) 1958 (ii) 1980 ?
  c What are the main causes of the increase in carbon dioxide?
  d Which countries or regions are the main sources of coal?
  e Why do you think it will be difficult to persuade these sources of coal to cut back on production?

3   **a** What are the expected consequences if the level of carbon dioxide doubles in the next century?
  b Study **F**. Compare the consequences of the greenhouse effect with the consequences of a little ice age. Which would have the more serious results?
  c Why is it not possible for us to accurately predict future climate?

49 : Acid Rain

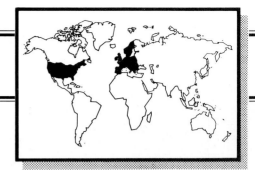

DESPITE LAWS in countries such as Britain and the United States, air pollution is still a problem in all of the world's major urban-industrial regions. The main air pollutants are:

- sulphur dioxide from power stations, industry and agriculture;
- nitrogen oxides from power stations, vehicles and industry;
- hydrocarbons from industrial processes and vehicles.

These gases react chemically with sunlight. The resultant **photochemical smog (B)** is a foul-smelling yellowish haze rich in ozone. It causes running eyes and noses, coughing and sometimes death, as well as severe damage to buildings and vegetation.

The Acid Rain Problem (E)   Air pollution does not only affect the urban-industrial centres where it is created. Chimneys up to 400 metres high disperse the gases, but they come to ground between 5 and 20 km distant and may then be blown to rural areas and even to foreign countries. Since the early 1970's, scientists have become very concerned about the effects of acid rain on natural ecosystems.

Rainfall is always slightly acidic (about pH 5) due to dissolved carbon dioxide and other naturally occurring acids in the atmosphere. Peak acidity for UK rainfall has been recorded in Pitlochry, Scotland at pH 2.4, 1,000 times more acidic than normal rain. Similar levels have been measured in Scandinavia and North America. Acidity is most serious in mountain regions where rainfall is much higher.

Buckingham Palace (1.6 km)

Hilton International Hotel (2.2 km)

Royal Albert Hall (4.1 km)

28th AUG 1981

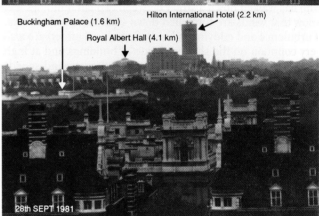

28th SEPT 1981

B Photochemical smog in London

The Effects of Acid Rain

- Thin soils beneath moorland or pine forest are naturally acid, but levels of acidity are worsened by acid rain. The acidity of rainwater flowing into streams and lakes is reduced by rocks containing calcium which neutralises the acid. Rocks such as granite, which contain little calcium, do not neutralise acid rain, so the acids enter rivers and destroy the ecosystem.

  The productivity of fisheries is reduced when water acidity is below pH 5.5, and fish deaths occur below pH5. Many lakes in Scandinavia and North America which once contained fish are now dead.
- Acid rainwater releases aluminium from the soil. This is poisonous to fish and plants.
- Trees are dying over much of Europe. The hot, dry summers of 1983 and 1984 seem to have triggered the decline, but also to blame is the acid rain which destroys the soils and tree roots.

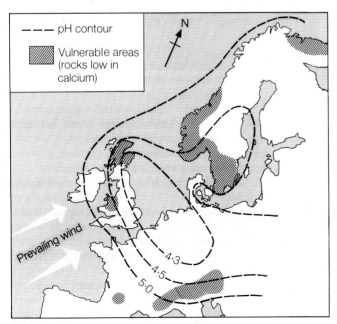

- - - pH contour

▨ Vulnerable areas (rocks low in calcium)

Prevailing wind

4.3
4.5
5.0

A Acid rain in Europe 1979

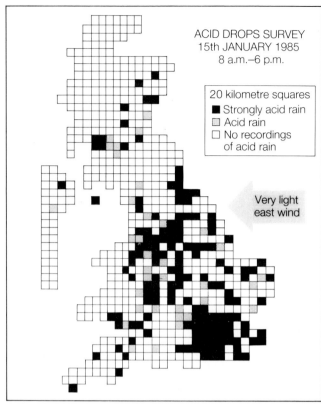

C Acid rain in Britain

- Buildings, gravestones and statues made of stone, particularly limestone, are eaten away as the stone dissolves. Repairing or replacing the damaged stone costs millions of pounds every year.

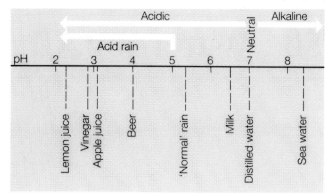

D The pH scale of acidity

What Action Should Be Taken? Not everyone agrees that industrial air pollution should be immediately ended. Here is a typical argument:

'Sulphur dioxide emissions have fallen in Britain by 40% since 1970. It is not clear that a further sudden reduction in emissions will have much effect. Neither is it clear that acid rain causes tree deaths and acid lakes. Plant disease, dry summers and planting of conifers may also be to blame. It would cost up to £160 million for each power station to install sulphur dioxide filters, which would raise the price of electricity by at least 5%. Nitrogen oxide emissions would not be reduced – every boiler would have to be modified to do this.

We recommend that more time be taken over this problem. New technology and more nuclear power will gradually reduce emissions. Meanwhile, we can continue adding lime to our affected lakes.'

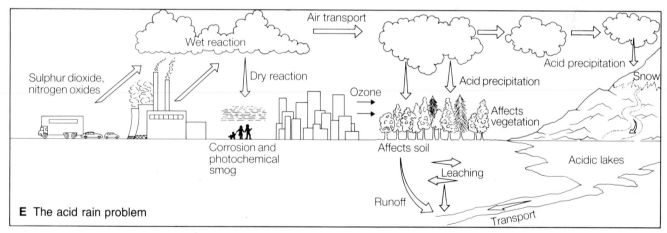

E The acid rain problem

1 Study **D**. What are the pH values for:
   • distilled water • normal rain • apple juice • acid rain
   • water acid enough to kill fish?
2 **a** What is the difference between smog and photochemical smog?
   b What harmful effects are produced by • photochemical smog • acid rain?

3 Study **A** and **C**.
   a Which areas of western Europe receive rain with the highest acidity?
   b Suggest reasons for this distribution of acid rain.
   c Which areas of Britain had strongly acid rain on 15 January 1985?
   d Why do some areas of Britain suffer less than others?
   e How would the pattern of acid rain change with a strong SW wind?
   f Britain accounts for one sixth of all the sulphur deposited in Norway. Explain how this is possible.
4 Read the opinion at the end of the section. Do you agree or disagree with it? Explain your answer.

101

50 : Water for All

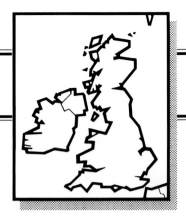

ONE OF OUR MOST important needs is a regular supply of clean, fresh water. We are lucky in Britain because our moist, maritime climate ensures a plentiful supply of rain to feed our rivers and reservoirs. However, during the dry summer of 1976, we did experience a taste of conditions in drought-stricken countries. As rivers and reservoirs dried up, restrictions on water use were introduced. Many people had to queue for water from stand pipes in the street.

Most of the world is not as fortunate. Deserts and semi-deserts cover one third of the world's land surface. Many other regions suffer from long dry seasons and unreliable rainfall. In developing countries, more than 90% of the available water may be used for farming rather than household or industrial use.

Meeting The Demand

Water demand in Britain is rising by 3% a year. Each family uses an average of 120 litres a day – about half a tonne! Industry uses huge amounts of water to make the things we need, though a lot of this water is recycled. It may take 40,000 litres to manufacture a car (**C**), but most of this can be re-used so that the amount consumed is only 5,000 litres.

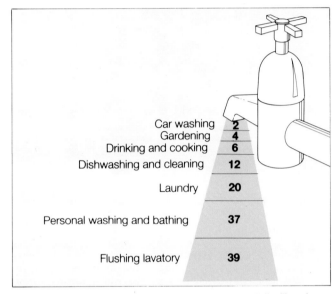

Car washing	2
Gardening	4
Drinking and cooking	6
Dishwashing and cleaning	12
Laundry	20
Personal washing and bathing	37
Flushing lavatory	39

B Average amount of water each person uses daily (litres)

Power stations are the largest users – about one quarter of all water is used for cooling the generators, but almost all of it goes back into the rivers. Altogether nearly 29 million litres of water (roughly the contents of a large reservoir) are supplied every day in England and Wales for household use, agriculture and industry.

Most of our water comes from rivers and reservoirs, though one-third is extracted from wells and boreholes. Underground water is stored in porous rocks known as **aquifers**. Rocks such as sandstone and chalk act like giant sponges, soaking up rainwater in their pores and fissures. Wells and boreholes give access to the water which can rise naturally or be pumped to the surface.

Water in rivers is lost to the water supply system unless dams are built to store it in reservoirs. These can also be used to maintain river flow when it would otherwise be too low for towns and cities downstream to take out their water supplies.

Unfortunately, the areas with heaviest rainfall are often not the same as the areas with highest water demand. As demand increases, particularly in areas where population is growing and new industries are developing, new sources of water have to be found.

Two ways of meeting increased demand is to build more and more reservoirs or extract more from underground sources. This is not always easy. Suitable sites for reservoirs and barrages (dams) across estuaries and bays such as the Wash are not very common, and the water table may fall if underground extraction is greater than rainfall can replace.

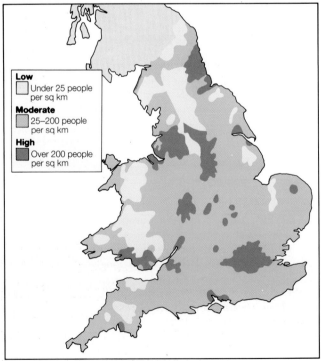

Low
☐ Under 25 people per sq km

Moderate
☐ 25–200 people per sq km

High
☐ Over 200 people per sq km

A Water demand in England and Wales based on population density

Far and away the biggest user of water is industry. Just how much water does go into the various production processes? Here are some figures calculated by officials of the Water Resources Board and the Nature Conservancy.

One litre of petrol takes over 70 litres to refine

One tonne of steel requires 44,000 litres

One kilogramme of rayon requires 1000 litres in manufacture

One kilogramme of artificial silk requires nearly 700 litres

To make one tyre requires 190,000 litres

180 litres is used in making a bag of cement

A four door family-size car requires over 40,000 litres to manufacture

350 litres of water is used in making one litre of beer

190 litres is used in making the paper for each copy of The Observer newspaper

A bag of coke takes 13,500 litres

One tonne of aluminium takes 1,350,000 litres

C Where does all the water go?

Another idea is to build new reservoirs in sparsely populated upland areas where rainfall is much higher. The water can then be transported long distances to areas of high demand by man-made aqueducts and by rivers. There are disadvantages, however. The cost of such developments in England and Wales has been put at £1,500 million (**D**). Local people are often unhappy to see their land flooded in order to supply water to people living in a distant part of the country. Conservationists object to the disappearance of attractive valleys, and habitats for rare plants and wildlife.

1 a What are the main sources of water for public use?
b What is an aquifer?
c How is water obtained from these aquifers?
2 a Using the statistics in **B**, calculate what percentage of total water use is used in each way.
b How much water does the average family use in one year?
c If there was a serious drought like that of 1976, make a list of measures you would introduce in order to save water at home.
d Which industries are the main water consumers?
e Why are the statistics in **B** not a true picture of water consumption by industry?
f Give two reasons why water consumption is rising.
3 Study **A** and **D**, and **C** in unit 26.
a Which parts of England and Wales have i) the highest rainfall ii) the highest demand?
b Suggest any problems this causes.
c Explain how a shortfall in supply might be overcome.
d Are there any disadvantages in introducing your solution? If so, explain what they are.

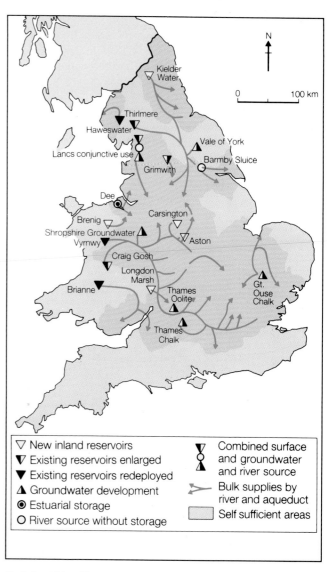

D A £1,500 million strategy for water

51 : Water Down the Drain

OVER 70% OF THE WORLD'S people have no supply of clean drinking water. Few have a tap or even a well. For most of them, water has to be carried from ponds or rivers after long walks. The same river or pond is often used for bathing and washing clothes as well as by animals.

Over half the deaths and illnesses in developing countries are caused by polluted water. In poorer countries less than half of the population has access to safe drinking water or facilities for sewage disposal. Conditions are usually worst in rural areas.

Dirty water is the carrier of diseases such as cholera, typhoid and dysentery. Perhaps 80% of all disease in the world is water-related. The result is that 50 million people die every year from water-borne diseases. In countries without a regular supply of clean water, life expectancy is between 40 and 50 compared with 70 or more in developed countries. Yet water-borne diseases can be wiped out by the introduction of clean, piped water supplies and proper sanitation.

The cost of providing standpipes, toilets, sewers and other necessary facilities to ensure acceptable water standards everywhere in the world has been estimated at $200,000,000,000! However, a start can be made if local people dig deep wells which do not dry out in periods of drought, and store water in small reservoirs (**A**).

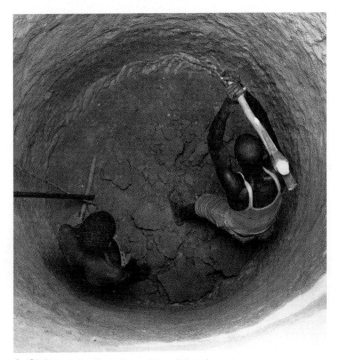

A Sinking a well on the edge of the desert

Water Treatment

In developed countries such as Britain, huge sums are spent each year on ensuring a regular supply of clean water. Supplies from reservoirs and boreholes are usually of good quality, but river water has to be filtered. Chemicals are added to improve taste or control possible smells, or alter the hardness or softness of the water. Chlorine is also added to kill any remaining harmful bacteria.

Our used water is often cleaned and recycled instead of wasted. Much of London's drinking water has already passed through several people before it reaches the city! Purification takes place in sewage works where wastes are broken down by bacteria and other tiny organisms. When the solid sludge is removed, the clean water is returned to rivers for use by someone living downstream. Sludge may be dumped at sea, used as farm fertiliser or burnt.

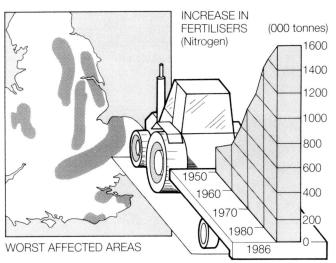

B Nitrate pollution and use by farmers

The Nitrate Problem Not all substances are removed from water by sewage treatment. These include toxic chemicals discharged accidentally by factories, and fertilisers such as nitrates which are washed from fields into streams. Such chemicals build up in rivers, lakes and aquifers, creating a health risk. About a million people in Britain receive tap water from underground sources with nitrate content above the EEC recommended level (**B**).

Dying Rivers In some parts of Britain, sewage systems are old and overloaded. Until money is found for new treatment works, raw sewage and waste from factories are pumped into rivers and estuaries.

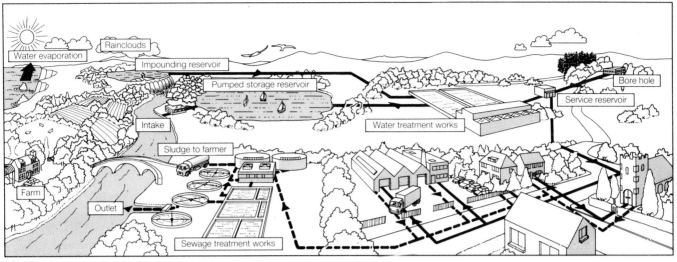

C The human water cycle

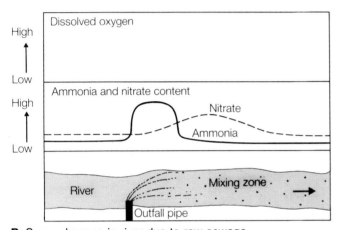

D Some changes in river due to raw sewage

E River quality in England & Wales (% of river length)

Water Authority	Good	Doubtful	Poor	Bad
Anglian	58	32	9	0.2
Northumbrian	87	10	2	0.8
North West	61	17	17	5
Severn–Trent	54	33	12	1
Southern	75	22	2	0.2
South West	66	27	6	0.6
Thames	65	28	7	0.1
Welsh	83	11	6	0.6
Wessex	61	32	6	0.6
Yorkshire	77	12	8	3
England & Wales	68	22	9	2

Unpolluted water is rich in dissolved oxygen for living plants and creatures to breathe. When sewage appears, bacteria start to break it down, just as they do in a sewage works. Unfortunately, the bacteria use up the oxygen needed by river life. Bacteria turn the sewage into ammonia, then into nitrates, which act as a fertiliser. Green pond weed and algae grow rapidly until they form a surface coating like green pea soup. Sunlight is blocked by this coating, so most river plants die and decay, using up still more oxygen. If this happens in enough places, a river may die.

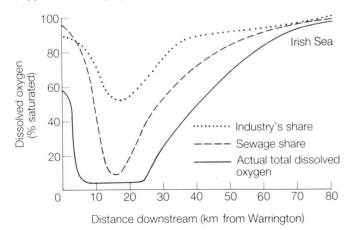

F Loss of dissolved oxygen in Mersey Estuary during a dry summer

1   **a** What are the main water-borne diseases?
b Suggest how clean water could be provided cheaply in developing countries.
c How were water-borne diseases like cholera wiped out in Britain?

2   **a** Copy **D**. Draw a line graph in the space provided to show how amount of dissolved oxygen in the river varies.
b According to **F**, what is the main reason for the lack of dissolved oxygen in the Mersey estuary?
c Study **E**. Which region of England and Wales has the cleanest rivers?
d Which region of England and Wales has the greatest problem of polluted rivers?
e Explain your answers to **c** and **d**. An atlas may help.

3   **a** What has happened to the use of nitrate fertilisers since 1950?
b Where are the areas most affected by nitrates in the water?
c Explain why these areas are worst affected.

4   Draw and label a series of four diagrams to show how clean water can lose nearly all life after large amounts of untreated sewage have been added.

5   Describe and explain the human water cycle in **C**.

105

52 : All at Sea

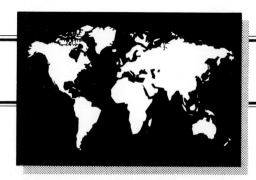

NEARLY THREE-QUARTERS of Earth's surface is water. Most of this is more than 1 km deep, but the areas of greatest economic importance are the shallow **continental shelves** on the fringes of the continents. These areas receive warmth, sunlight and abundant supplies of food which enable fish and other marine life to breed.

Overfishing

Modern trawlers and inshore boats are equipped with echo-sounders and depth sounders to locate shoals of fish. They can refrigerate their catches and stay at sea for long periods. Instead of waiting for the fish to migrate, boats now follow them to their breeding grounds. Giant factory ships may wait to process catches brought in by the local fishermen. Sizes of net mesh have become smaller, enabling smaller, younger fish to be caught. The result is a fall in fish stocks as they are caught faster than they can breed and replace their numbers. Once stocks have run out, fishermen change to new species or try to find new grounds.

Overfishing has already affected at least 25 of the world's major fishing grounds. The worst affected grounds are near the leading industrial nations. In European waters, herring numbers declined so much that a total ban was declared from 1977–84, while catches of cod, haddock and mackerel have been seriously reduced through falling stocks (**A**). The people of Iceland were so worried about their cod stocks that they fought three Cod Wars against Britain in order to set up a 200 mile (320 km) fishing limit.

Worst of all was the case of the Peruvian anchovy. In the 1960's it accounted for one fifth of the world's fish catch. It was mostly used as fishmeal for livestock and fertiliser. Repeated overfishing combined with a shift in ocean currents led to a collapse in numbers.

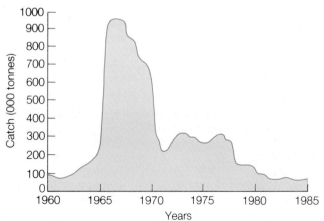

A Catches of mackerel 1960–85 in European waters

B Outfall of untreated sewage onto the beach at Mount's Bay, Penzance.

Pollution

The continental shelves eg North Sea, are the busiest sea areas in the world. Apart from shipping, fishing and oil exploration, they cater for tourists and holidaymakers. They are also a dump for all kinds of waste from the large cities and industrial centres nearby.

In many places, raw sewage is poured straight into the sea through pipes (**B**), polluting bathing waters and beaches. Sewage sludge from treatment works, often rich in nutrients and heavy metals, is also dumped out to sea. When oil tankers wash out their tanks or run aground, they can cause oil slicks which contaminate beaches and kill wildlife.

More important are the direct discharges from coastal cities and industries, and the input from major rivers **C**. Nutrients rich in phosphate and nitrogen have resulted in increased activity by bacteria and plankton. These need oxygen to break down the nutrients, so some sea areas are now becoming biologically empty through lack of oxygen.

More than 10,000 different industrial chemicals enter the ocean. Many of these cannot be broken down by bacteria, so they build up in sediments on the sea floor and enter the food chain. This was shown in the Japanese village of Minamata, where mercury waste from a nearby factory built up in plankton, shellfish, fish and, finally, people. Poisoning among local fishing families killed 43 people and left more than 700 permanently disabled.

Other problems include dumping of waste from mines and nuclear plants, and burning of toxic chemicals at sea. The Irish Sea receives low-level radioactive discharges from Sellafield in Cumbria, though high-level waste is no longer dumped at sea.

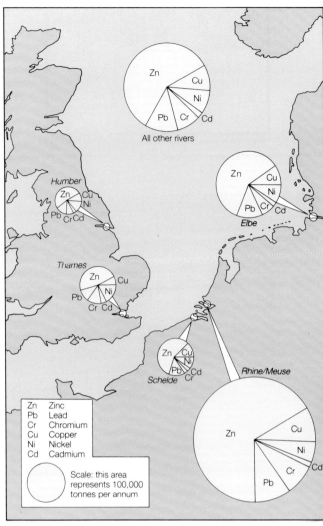

C Metals brought to the North Sea by rivers

Bathers beware: coast is not clear

TESTS on 2,000 litres of water from around the Italian coast are likely to give holidaymakers the shivers.

Samples collected in the past few weeks by the crew of the Goletta Verde, a yacht co-owned by the news magazine L'Espresso and an environmental association, are expected to confirm that large stretches of the Italian coast are dangerously polluted by industrial or domestic waste.

However, not all the Goletta Verde's findings were bad. It has discovered and mapped Italy's last stretches of glorious clear blue sea.

But first the bad news. Hotels on the Adriatic are still plagued by ugly banks of seaweed flourishing in water high in phosphates. The ugliest consequence of this type of pollution is dead fish washed up on the beach.

Other nasty substances located included: arsenic near Bari; nitrates, mercury and solvents near Brindisi; lead and fuel near ports such as Reggio Calabria; mercury near Rosignano in Tuscany and almost everything in the Gulf of Naples, considered an emergency zone by the Italian government.

Even the sea off the tourist spots of Amalfi and Positano contained chemical pollutants. And only the very brave should swim on beaches at the mouth of the Tiber near Rome, where the principal culprit is raw sewage.

In northern Italy the pollution is primarily industrial, while in the south tracts of clean sea alternate with very dirty water as seaside towns pump out raw sewage.

Now for some bathing tips: as a general rule avoid built-up areas or mouths of rivers, particularly in the south. On the northwest coast you may find what you are looking for at Portofino, or along an unspoilt tract of the Ligurian coast. Elba is fine, and so, on the whole, is southern Tuscany. Skip Rome. By San Felice di Circeo you are doing fine.

Official confirmation of the situation came from a health ministry report last month which estimated that 400 kilometres of coast were dangerously polluted by industrial or domestic waste. It linked the high incidence of typhus in the south to shellfish from the polluted areas.

D Tourism and coastal pollution in Italy

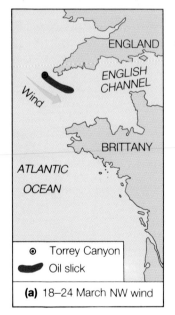

E Oil slicks from the Torrey Canyon

1 **a** What are continental shelves?
   b Why are continental shelves so rich in fish?
   c In which year was the peak catch of mackerel in European waters?
   d How many tonnes of mackerel were caught in that year?
   e Explain why the mackerel catch dropped so suddenly.
2 **a** Study **C**. Which is the most common metal entering the North Sea?
   b Which river system delivers most metals to the North Sea?
   c Why is the metal pollution greatest from the river system named in **b**? (An atlas may help)
   d Draw a simple food chain to show the cause of Minamata disease.
3 Read **D**. Imagine you are Italian Minister for Tourism. Write a report in two sections, summarising (i) the causes of pollution and the problems resulting from pollution, (ii) your recommendations for reducing damage to tourism.
4 **a** Study **E**. Draw two outline maps of the same coast. Add the positions of the Torrey Canyon oil slicks at the end of the following periods, assuming the ship is still leaking:
   (i) 26 March–7 April, NW wind. Average drift rate 5 km per day.
   (ii) 8–12 April, NE wind. Average drift rate 20 km per day.
   b List the problems that faced the local people after 18 March.

107

53 : Harnessing the Power of the Atom

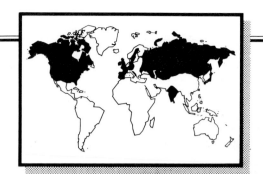

AS THE WORLD'S population grows and people expect a higher standard of living, the demand for energy also increases. Energy demand is predicted to rise by between 25 and 30% in developed countries from 1980 to 2000. In developing countries it is expected to double over the same period.

This has led to forecasts of a world energy crisis during the next century. Until now, fossil fuels have accounted for about 90% of the world's energy consumption (A), but many countries are looking for alternative sources of energy for the future. The leading candidate for future energy supply is nuclear power.

How Is Nuclear Power Produced? Nuclear power stations use heat obtained from atoms of uranium or plutonium when they are split in the core of a reactor. This process is controlled by a cooling system around the core. The cooling system may use water, or gases such as carbon dioxide. Heat from the reactor is used to make steam and this steam is used to turn the turbines which are linked to electricity generators.

C Wylfa nuclear power station

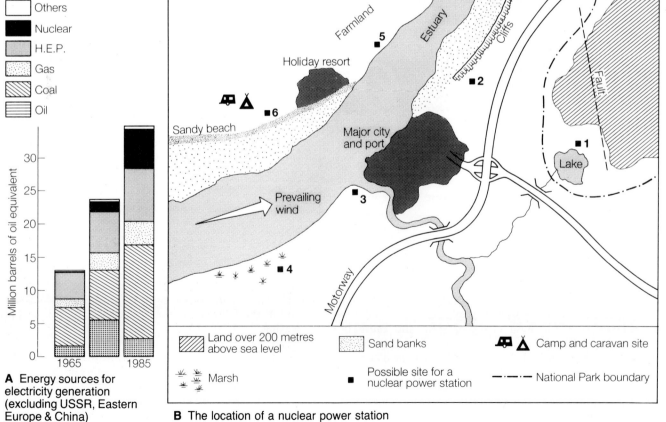

A Energy sources for electricity generation (excluding USSR, Eastern Europe & China)

B The location of a nuclear power station

What Are the Advantages?

- Uranium is a cheap, easily available mineral. The main producing countries are the USA, Australia, Canada, South Africa and Niger.
- Uranium is energy intensive: one small pellet of uranium contains as much energy as a tonne of coal or four barrels of oil.
- Energy from nuclear power can be cheaper than burning fossil fuels.
- Nuclear power is clean – there are no ash or toxic gases to pollute the air and to cause acid rain.
- The large number of overseas uranium suppliers means that nuclear stations are less likely to be put out of action by strikes. Nuclear stations kept producing during the 1986 miners' strike in Britain.
- New types of nuclear reactor, called **fast breeders**, are expected to produce plutonium as a by-product. This means they could produce their own fuel, a very cheap method of energy production! Even more advanced **fusion reactors** are being researched. These could use energy from joining atoms of hydrogen – their fuel would be water!

What Are The Disadvantages?

- Nuclear power stations are very expensive to build: the new station at Sizewell in Suffolk will cost at least £1.5 billion.
- There are few sites suitable for their location – they need to have firm foundations. Nuclear power stations in areas of unstable crust could release radioactivity if an earthquake caused damage to the reactor. They also need plenty of cooling water. Early stations were built away from large urban areas for safety.
- Highly radioactive waste is produced. This has to be stored in water until it can be sent by rail to a reprocessing plant at Sellafield in Cumbria, but it remains very dangerous for thousands of years.
- There are few places suitable for the disposal of nuclear waste. Most countries propose to bury it in deep mines or shafts. Less radioactive waste is also buried on land or at sea.
- Some people are very unhappy about living near nuclear power stations or waste dumps. The inquiry into a new station at Sizewell took nearly 5 years. Similar public protests are likely in future.
- The stations will be very difficult and expensive to make safe when they come to the end of their active lives after 25 to 30 years. The cost of dismantling each station is put at £2.7 billion.
- They are a security risk. Terrorists could steal plutonium to make a nuclear bomb, or take over a station in a blackmail attempt.
- Nuclear power is not always cheaper. The price of fossil fuels has fallen by 40% since 1985, making them a cheaper source of electricity.
- There is always the slight threat of a major accident eg the Chernobyl disaster of 1986 (see unit 59). Failproof equipment and highly trained staff are essential.

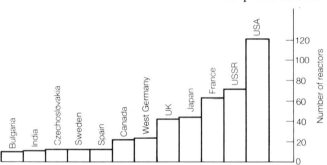

D Main countries with nuclear reactors in operation or under contstruction, 1986

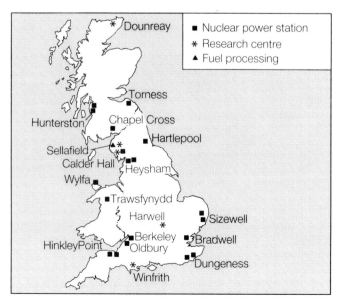

E British nuclear establishments

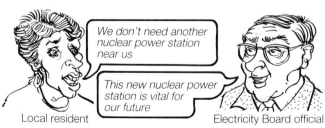

1 Study D.
   a Which country has the most nuclear reactors?
   b Which is the only developing country on the graph?
   c Why do you think only one developing country is on the graph?

2 **a** Why do experts predict an energy crisis in the next century?
   b Roughly what fraction of world electricity came from nuclear power in 1985?
   c Briefly describe what **A** shows about changes in world electricity generation since 1965.

3 From the lists of advantages and disadvantages above, choose the points you think these people would use to support their views.

We don't need another nuclear power station near us

Local resident

This new nuclear power station is vital for our future

Electricity Board official

4 **a** Study E. Where are nearly all British nuclear stations located?
   b What is the main reason for this location?
   c Copy **B**. Select the location you think is most suitable for a new nuclear power station. Explain your answer.

109

54 : Living on the Fault Line

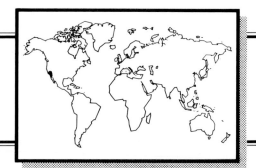

THE STATE of California has long acted as a magnet for immigrants from the rest of the United States and overseas, due to its pleasant climate, rich resources of land and minerals, magnificent scenery and good job prospects. Today its population has reached 25 million, almost half the number of people in Britain. But there is one major disadvantage of living in 'The Sunshine State' – the threat of a devastating earthquake.

The entire state is criss-crossed by a maze of faults, any one of which can suddenly slip to cause an earthquake. The main threat, however, is the San Andreas Fault, a giant fracture in the crust which separates two plates moving in opposite directions. This fault passes close to the densely-populated urban belt which follows the coast between San Francisco and San Diego.

The worst recorded earthquake in California struck the city of San Francisco just after 5 am on 18 April 1906. The crust suddenly shifted by about 6 metres, generating a shock measuring 8.3 on the Richter scale. Worst hit were the brick or stone buildings which stood on soft sediment. Wooden structures on solid bedrock remained standing. Many of these were destroyed afterwards, however, when fire spread through much of the city. Fractured gas and water mains made the job of the firefighters more difficult, forcing them to use water from the bay. Firebreaks were made by dynamiting buildings.

San Francisco was rebuilt. Today there are more than 6 million people living around San Francisco Bay. A similar number live around Los Angeles, 600 km to the south. Experts suggest that both cities are under threat from a major quake within the next 30 years as stress builds up along the fault. The factors which make a disaster likely include:

- thousands of old brick buildings in Los Angeles which could be death traps for 200,000 people;
- Californians rely heavily on road transport. Motorway overpasses would collapse in a major quake, bringing road transport to a standstill;

Quakes show cracks in the California lifestyle

From Ivor Davies

Los Angeles

When a Los Angeles television station recently offered its viewers a free Earthquake Survival Guide, it thought the response was good. Some 50,000 booklets went out in nine months.

Last month alone, however, the station despatched 15,000 more, and it is sending out additional booklets at the rate of 250 a day.

What happened in the interim was a series of jolting earthquakes, more frequent than California has ever experienced, bringing in their wake more than 100 aftershocks.

All the shaking has turned the state's 25 million population, normally quite sanguine when it comes to earthquakes, into a jittery mass which jumps at every sonic boom, stops in its tracks every time a neighbour's dog howls and stockpiles food, water and medical supplies as if anticipating a global conflagration.

Life in California has always been lived on the edge. As we sit by our swimming pools, shaded by our palm trees, cooled by the gentle breezes from the Pacific, while the rest of the country swelters in a drought, we understand deep in our Puritan hearts that one day we will have to pay the price for paradise.

That day, some of the experts now tell us, could be coming sooner than we think.

The latest cluster of earthquakes began on July 8, when a jolt registering six on the Richter scale hit the desert resort town of Palm Springs.

Within days it was followed by one measuring 5.3 centred in the Pacific off the beach community of Oceanside.

That in turn was followed by a series of tremors in the mountainous area near Bishop, culminating in one of 6.1 centred in the Chalfont valley.

Damage was moderate and injuries mostly minor. None of the tremors, however, occurred on the notorious San Andreas Fault line, which runs through California from north of San Francisco almost to the US-Mexican border town of El Centro.

The entire state is criss-crossed by a crazy quilt of fault lines, but it is the San Andreas, the experts predict, which will send us "the big one", wreaking the kind of havoc visited on Mexico City last autumn.

What seems to be disturbing the population here even more than the prospect of the earth beneath their feet going into spasms is the gradually dawning knowledge that the so-called experts do not seem to know any more about predicting earthquakes than the people to whom they are preaching.

Do these tremors portend another, more massive upheaval? Maybe, say the experts.

The truth seems to be that, apart from inviting us to be prepared, the seismologists can agree only that the big one is coming sometime within the next 30 to 50 years.

A Earthquakes in California

- likely breakdowns in communications and power supplies. Emergency services would be affected, particularly since some of them are located on or near fault lines. Computer systems would not operate;
- over 200 major dams and reservoirs in California. Many are vulnerable to collapse. Many thousands could be drowned;
- the large number of nuclear power stations and storage sites for nuclear weapons in the state, which could release radioactivity into the air and soil. Oil storage sites near harbours are likely to catch fire.

The Threat To San Francisco The death toll would vary according to the time of day. This is one official estimate for the San Francisco area:

2.30 am Most people asleep in their homes. The dams hold. Death toll: 3,000. Injured: 11,000.

2 pm Many people at work. Streets and pavements busy. Dams hold. Death toll; 9,500. Injured: 35,000.

4.30 pm Rush hour. Streets and pavements crowded. Dams hold. Death toll over 10,000. Injured: 40,000. If the dams also failed, the toll of dead and injured could reach 100,000.

C Aerial view of San Andreas Fault

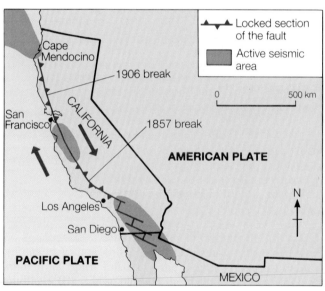

B The San Andreas Fault and California earthquakes

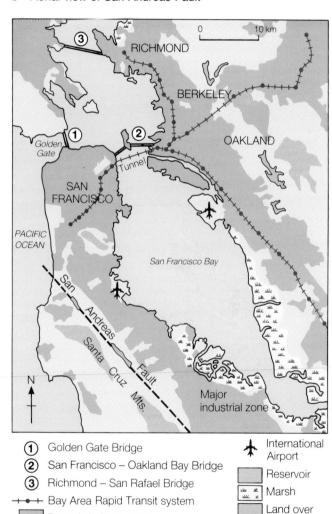

① Golden Gate Bridge
② San Francisco – Oakland Bay Bridge
③ Richmond – San Rafael Bridge
+•+ Bay Area Rapid Transit system
☐ Densely built-up areas

✈ International Airport
☐ Reservoir
☐ Marsh
☐ Land over 300 m

D San Francisco conurbation

1 Study **B**, then answer the following questions.
a Which two crustal plates are separated by the San Andreas Fault?
b What type of fault is the San Andreas? (see unit 8).
c How long is the fault system north-south?
d Which sections of the fault are slowly creeping and causing small earthquakes?
e Which sections of the fault are most likely to cause a major earthquake in the future? Explain your answer.
2 Study **A** and **D**.
a How many people live in California?
b Why is the San Francisco area so densely populated?
c Describe the types of disaster which might follow an earthquake in this area. Give evidence from **D**.

d When is the next big earthquake expected to occur?
e Why are the people of California prepared to risk a major earthquake?
f What were the main causes of the destruction of San Francisco in 1906?
g Why might the authorities not want to order a mass evacuation after advance warning of an earthquake?
h What actions, other than evacuation, could be taken by the authorities to reduce the impact of an earthquake in San Francisco?

111

55 : Locating a Settlement

PEOPLE throughout the world live in settlements which vary in size from a lone family farm to a conurbation with a population of many millions. People originally settled in all of these places because there were certain advantages to living there.

The Early Settlers

The place where people choose to locate their settlement is called its **site**. The needs of early settlers were simple:

- A source of timber for fuel and building material. Natural stone could also be used for building.
- Reasonably fertile land for growing crops and raising livestock.
- A dry site above flood level but close to a source of clean water such as a spring or well.
- A good defensive position in case of attack.
- A sheltered position less exposed to cold winds.

In England, nearly every village that exists today had been founded by the time of the Domesday Survey of 1086. Many villages were located on rivers or streams which provided a source of water, fish, power for mills, and a means of transport.

Settlers did not always find an ideal site. It was clearly difficult to find a good defensive site on a hill which was also sheltered. One answer was to locate the settlement on lower ground but close to a fortified hill which could be used for refuge during an attack eg Edinburgh, Durham. Another answer was to take advantage of a river meander (bend) or marsh as a natural line of defence eg Shrewsbury, Ely.

As trade became more important in the Middle Ages, route centres expanded rapidly into market towns. These settlements were located at crossroads, near river fords or bridging points, and on estuaries. Sources of raw materials

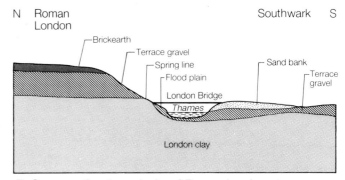

B Cross-section through site of Roman London

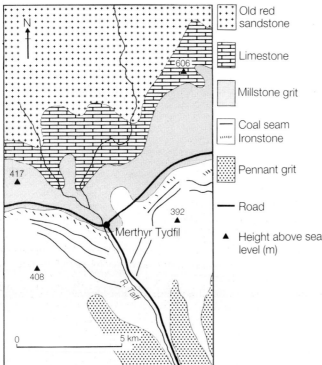

A Location of Merthyr Tydfil

Legend for map A:
- Old red sandstone
- Limestone
- Millstone grit
- Coal seam / Ironstone
- Pennant grit
- Road
- ▲ Height above sea level (m)

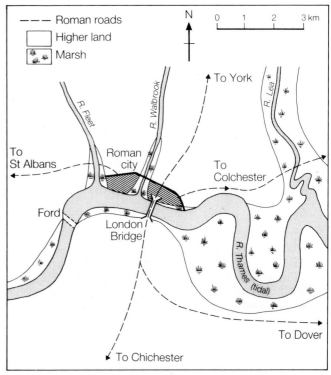

C The site of Roman London

were another attraction, especially fuels such as coal, metals such as copper, lead and zinc, and valuable minerals such as gold or silver. New settlements grew up almost overnight, although Britain saw nothing like the gold rushes in California or Alaska.

The Industrial Revolution of the 18th century began with water power. Many mill towns, notably in the Pennine foothills of Lancashire, owe their existence to the need for fast-flowing streams. The introduction of steam engines in the 19th century meant a switch to steam power based on burning coal. As mines and factories appeared all over the coalfields, people were drawn from the surrounding coun-

tryside in their millions. Small villages such as Leeds, Birmingham or Manchester suddenly expanded into major industrial centres. Coalmining settlements were built close to the pits, while towns such as Consett in County Durham and Ebbw Vale in South Wales owed their location and growth to the expanding iron and steel industry.

Even today, new settlements are being established in Britain. They are located near conurbations and major roads, often as a result of political decisions to attract people and industry from the overcrowded cities, or to bring jobs to areas of high unemployment (see unit 43).

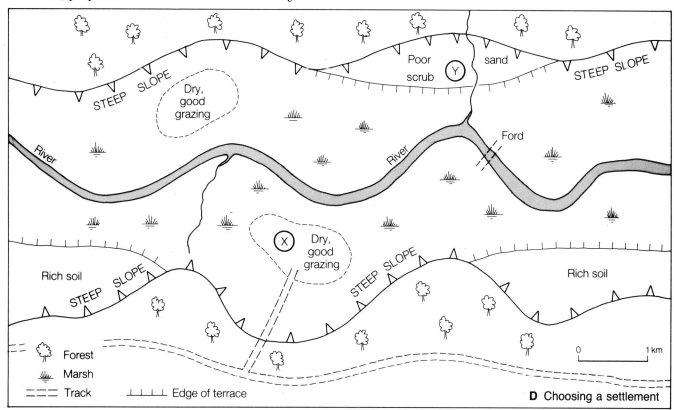

D Choosing a settlement

1 **a** Make a list of the main factors which have influenced the location of settlements.
   b Study A. Briefly explain why you think people settled in this location.
   c Why do some settlements no longer exist and become ghost towns?
2 **a** The Romans founded the city of London nearly 2000 years ago. Explain the location they chose (see **B** and **C**).

b Suggest why the Romans did not build their city on the south bank of the Thames at Southwark.
3 **a** D shows an unsettled area in Britain. The leaders of an Anglo-Saxon tribe cannot decide whether site X or site Y is more suitable for a village. As chief of the tribe, make the decision and justify it to your followers.
   b Now complete the table below (**E**). The weighting you choose ranges from 10 (most important) to 1 (least important). The site with the lowest total is seen as the most efficient and favourable.
   c Does your answer to **b** agree with your choice in **a**? If not, give possible reasons.

E Factors influencing settlement	Distance from		Weighting	Distance × weighting	
Resource	Site X	Site Y	(1–10)	Site X	Site Y
Water	1.0km	0.25km			
Arable	2.0km	2.5 km			
Grazing	0.1km	3.5 km			
Fuel	1.5km	0.75km			
Building Material	1.5km	0.75km			
Totals					

113

56 : The Aberfan Disaster

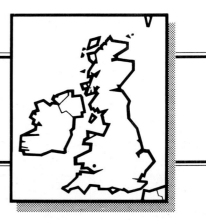

THE VILLAGE OF ABERFAN lies in the narrow valley of the River Taff (**A**). In the mid-19th century, the high quality coals of South Wales were much in demand, and coalmining began in the area around Merthyr Tydfil. Until then, Aberfan contained a few cottages, a public house and some scattered farmhouses. When the Merthyr Vale colliery opened in 1875, the mine owners built new terraced houses nearby to house miners and their families.

Prelude

Large amounts of waste are produced from collieries – about half a tonne of rock for every tonne of coal. Until the First World War, waste was dumped between the canal and the mountainside at Aberfan. However, the lack of space on the narrow valley floor led to tipping on the valley side. By 1966, there were seven tips towering above the village (**D**). Tip 7, the most recent, was the only one to contain fine particles called 'tailings' which passed through the coal filters.

Merthyr Mountain to the west of Aberfan has a fairly high annual rainfall, averaging about 1500mm. There are a number of streams and springs on the slope where the

tipping took place. The tips located here showed signs of instability on several occasions. In 1944, Tip 4 slid down the mountainside for a distance of 500m; the cause was never properly explained. A smaller slide of Tip 7 in 1963 was not made public. Tipping continued on the site of the slip.

The Disaster

There had been heavy rainfall on the mountain, but the morning of 21 October 1966 dawned sunny with mist in the valley. Men arriving for work on Tip 7 reported a large depression at the point of the tip. They were told that another site for tipping would be chosen. Then suddenly the tip began to flow down the slope like a huge wave. More than 100,000 cubic metres of soft, pasty mud rushed downhill at a speed of perhaps 30 km per hour (**B**).

Nearby farm cottages were buried first. All the occupants were killed. The flow continued over the disused canal and headed for the village. Lessons had just begun in the Pantglas Junior School. The mudflow struck without warning, killing five teachers and 109 children. As the flow came to rest on the valley floor, it demolished 18 houses and badly damaged 60 other buildings, including the senior

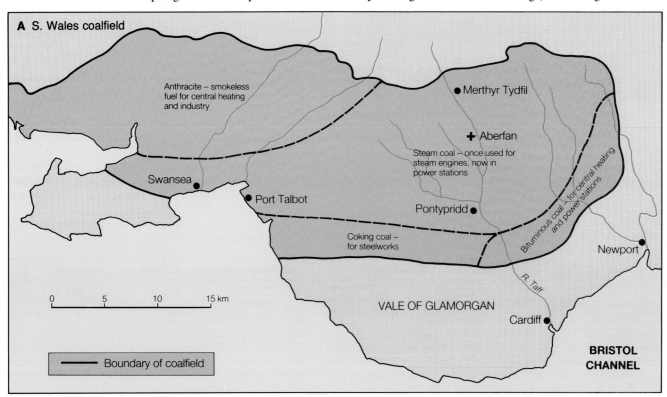

A S. Wales coalfield

Anthracite – smokeless fuel for central heating and industry

● Merthyr Tydfil

✚ Aberfan

Steam coal – once used for steam engines, now in power stations

● Swansea

● Port Talbot

Pontypridd ●

Bituminous coal – for central heating and power stations

Newport ●

Coking coal – for steelworks

R. Taff

VALE OF GLAMORGAN

Cardiff ●

BRISTOL CHANNEL

0   5   10   15 km

━━━ Boundary of coalfield

B The Aberfan debris flow, 1966

C Aberfan today. The white outline shows the area which was covered by the debris flow

school. Fortunately, the older pupils started school at 9.30, so most of them escaped. The final death toll was 144.

Aftermath

A public enquiry decided that the mudflow was due to a number of factors.

- Tipping on steep valley sides was recognised as very dangerous.
- A spring which emerged from the sandstone bedrock had caused erosion at the base of the tip, causing it to become unstable.
- Heavy rain had saturated the waste, reducing internal friction and increasing its weight.
- The instability may have been helped by the very fine tailings included in Tip 7.
- Earlier warnings had not been heeded, so that tipping had continued on sites already shown to be unstable by previous slips.

In 1968, the Aberfan tip complex was completely removed and landscaped (**C**). But there were another 1300 tips spread over the South Wales coalfield. The Coal Board began close monitoring of all tips and worked with local authorities to contour many disused tips, planting them with grass and trees. In places, such as the Aberdare Valley, lakes, walking trails and parkland have replaced the surface buildings and tips.

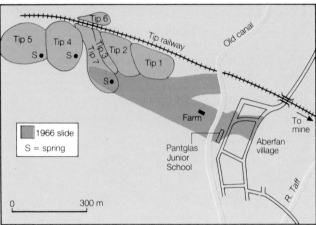

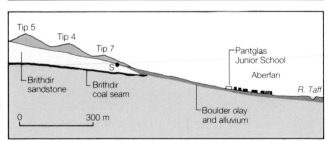

D The location of Aberfan and waste tips, 1966

1 **a** Explain why South Wales became one of the most important coalfields in Britain during the late 19th century.
b Imagine you are speaking to a foreign visitor. Describe the location of Aberfan giving as much detailed information as possible.
c Describe the function of Aberfan before the 1870's.
d Why was Aberfan expanded and by whom?

e What type of coal was mined at Merthyr Vale colliery in Aberfan?
2 **a** Why were waste tips necessary at Aberfan?
b How many waste tips were there near the village?
c Why was the waste tipped onto the mountainside?
d How was the waste carried up to the tips?
3 **a** What were the physical factors which led to the Aberfan disaster?
b What distance did the 1966 mudflow travel?
c List the factors which resulted in such a high death toll.
d To what extent do you think the Coal Board was to blame? Give reasons for your answer.
e What measures would you take to ensure that such a disaster never happens again?

115

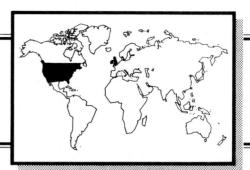

57 : Our Throwaway Society

OUR PLANET'S LIMITED resources are disappearing faster than ever. This is especially true in rich, developed countries, but as standards of living improve and population increases in developing countries, the day is coming ever nearer when vital resources such as oil will run out completely. The only hope is to recycle the rarer materials or find substitutes, just as concrete and plastics have replaced steel for many purposes.

The Nature of Waste Some 25 million tonnes of household waste are produced every year in Britain. In the United States, 400 million tonnes of industrial waste are generated annually in addition to nearly 200 million tonnes of household waste. Every one of us generates a huge amount of waste every week, most of it in some form of packaging. Estimates for New York State suggest that each person throws away 9 times their body weight every year. Somehow, the United States has to find ways of disposing of 7 million cars, 20 million tonnes of waste paper, 48 billion tin cans and 26 billion bottles.

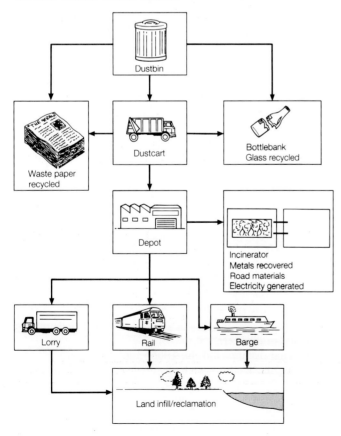

A Disposal of household waste

Waste Disposal

The most common method of waste disposal is simply to dump it in a disused pit or quarry (**D**). Many coastal marshes or mud flats have also been reclaimed in this way. There are 5,000 such tips in Britain, and 90% of US waste is disposed of by tipping. Domestic and commercial refuse is usually deposited in layers three metres thick then covered with soil to minimise problems from flies, birds or rodents. As layer upon layer of rubbish builds up, it slowly rots away, producing methane gas. After a suitable time, the old tip can be landscaped and used for recreation or building.

Not everyone is happy with this method. Methane gas is explosive and dangerous. Solvents and other chemicals in common household use can be leached out of the tip so that they contaminate underlying groundwater. Many plastics do not rot away, but survive intact for centuries. Finally, so much waste is being generated that suitable sites for dumping are running out, and the cost of buying sites is rising rapidly.

B

Germans build a paper mountain

**From Anna Tomforde
in Bonn**

FIRST there was Chernobyl. Then there was the Rhine pollution. Now it's the Great Unrecycled Paper Mountain. All in all, 1986 has been a bad year for West Germany, environmentally speaking.

For every bottle there is a bank. For every beer or soft drink can, there is a welcome and a future. Each month, on a date advertised in the local paper, collectors call (though never on Sundays) to take away the unwanted and the salvageable. On November 1, a new law sanctified the war on waste, stating that recycling should take priority over cost factors.

But when it comes to waste paper - 5 million tons this year - the system cannot cope. It is piling up on all sides.

This year, the Paper Mountain is set to grow to 800,000 tons.

But surveys have shown that the consumer who goes in for recycling to ease his conscience is not so enthusiastic about buying the recycled product. Each year, West Germans buy only about 130,000 tonnes of "grey" recycled paper, compared with 4.5 million tonnes of virgin white writing paper.

Rubbish-power saves fuel

Operators of the USSR's first rubbish-burning power plant, in Kharkov, the Ukraine, reckon they reclaim around a million cubic metres of fuel otherwise wasted each year.

Vadim Sirotenko, the brains behind the project, says that the plant also salvages 50 tons of metal a month, extracted from the ashes with a magnetic separator.

Other solids from the plant are used as additions to cement and asphalt, and the ash itself is used as a base for builders' plaster.

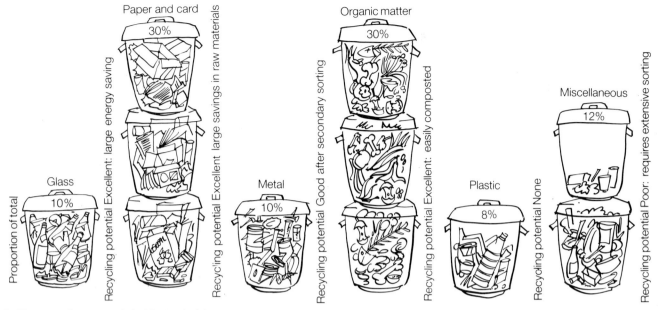

C The recycling potential of household waste

The other main alternative is incineration, which involves burning all refuse. In some cases, the heat is used in buildings or to generate electricity. However, the cost of building incinerators is high, while toxic smoke and gases result in air pollution.

Recycling

In order to conserve valuable raw materials, some domestic or industrial waste can be separated out and recycled. Glass bottles, metal cans, paper, plastic and fabric all have commercial value so that it may be worth spending money on processing them for re-use. The British government estimates that £750 million a year could be saved if waste materials could be reclaimed and reused. Or as one expert said, 'Simply recovering one edition of the New York Times would leave 75,000 trees standing.'

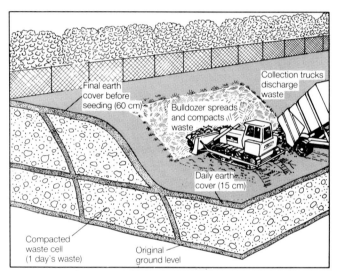

D Disposal of solid waste by landfill

1　a Study **C**. Draw a pie chart to show the proportions of each type of waste in the waste of an average household.
　b What is meant by recycling?
　c Why is mixed waste difficult to recycle?
　d When recycling is not possible, how else might resources be conserved?
2　a What is meant by a bottle bank?
　b What is meant by incineration?

c Explain how household waste is disposed of. (**A**)
d What happens when waste is dumped at a tip or infill? (**D**)
e What problems result from (i) tipping, (ii) incineration?
3　a Study the statistics in **E**. What has happened to the total waste generated in Greater London 1969–84?
　b Complete **E** by calculating the percentage of the total for each method of disposal in 1984.
　c What changes have taken place according to **E**?
4　a Study **B**. Briefly explain the good and bad points of the methods mentioned in each article.
　b Name the method of waste disposal you prefer and give reasons for your choice.

Year	1969	1974	1979	1984	% of total
Incineration	151	335	212	374	
Tipping	2,568	2,634	2,660	2,750	
Recycling	11	14	27	104	
Total	2,730	2,983	2,899	3,228	100

E Disposal of Refuse in Greater London (thousand tonnes)

58 : The Motorway: Menace or Necessity?

WHEN THE FIRST stretch of motorway in Britain was completed in 1959, there were 5 million cars and 1 million goods vehicles on the roads. Buses, coaches and railways accounted for 40% of all passenger journeys, but private cars were increasing in importance. Lorries were rapidly taking traffic away from the railways.

In 1987, there were nearly 17 million cars and 2 million goods vehicles on the roads. Meanwhile, the motorway network has expanded to more than 2,800 km (A). Although motorways account for only 0.8% of the total road network, they take 11.7% of the traffic.

The government built the motorways to meet increasing demand by road users, but the new roads helped to hasten the decline of the railways. Motorways were intended to help trade and industry by providing fast, direct routes between cities, ports and industrial centres. By avoiding narrow country roads, crossroads and traffic lights, and busy urban centres, journey times and costs were slashed, and road safety improved.

Motorways have encouraged the growth of fast, cheap, long-distance coach services and goods transport by juggernaut (lorries weighing up to 38 tonnes). They have also taken heavy traffic away from villages and unsuitable country roads. Industrial estates, new towns and giant shopping centres have been built beside motorways to take advantage of the good communications. The M25 ring road has recently been completed to take through traffic around London instead of allowing it to pass through the congested city centre.

Opposition to Motorways
- Motorways take up large amounts of land, particularly at junctions where several motorways meet eg Spaghetti Junction in Birmingham (C). This may be valuable, good quality farmland.
- Pleasant views and attractive scenery are destroyed by a motorway cutting across the landscape. Motorways can also affect local wildlife and split villages, farms or other property. In such cases, access can be made across the motorway for people and wildlife.
- Motorways attract more traffic. This increases traffic pressure on feeder roads. It also leads to traffic jams on both the motorways and their slip roads, particularly at weekends and peak commuting or holiday times. Accidents are more likely at such times.
- Motorways are very expensive to build – often over £1 million per kilometre – and construction disrupts local life for a year or more as hundreds of lorries and workers are brought in.
- Increased heavy traffic damages the motorway surface.

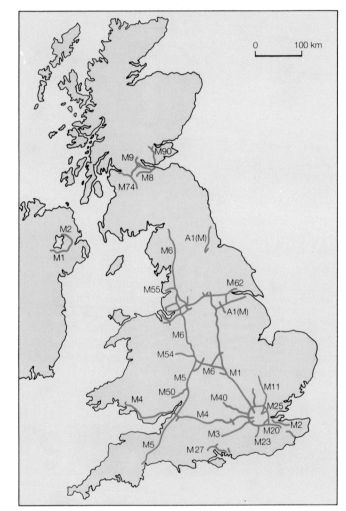

A Motorways in Britain (1986)

This means expensive repairs and traffic jams. There is also traffic noise and air pollution for people living nearby. Barriers or cuttings then have to be added to reduce noise levels.
- Lengthy, expensive public enquiries take place before a final route is chosen. However, land and property can be bought by the government under compulsory purchase if it lies along the final route, even if the owner has no wish to sell.
- Britain relies more on road transport than any other European country. Money might be better spent on modernising railways, canals and inland waterways than building new motorways.

118

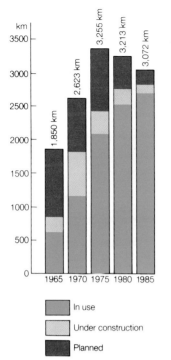

B Motorway progress

Key:
- In use
- Under construction
- Planned

C Spaghetti Junction near Birmingham

1 **a** When was the first stretch of motorway in Britain completed?
b During which five-year period was the greatest length of motorway constructed (see **B**)?
c Why were the motorways built?
d Describe the pattern of motorways shown on **A**.
e Why are there no motorways in large areas of the country?

2 **a** Draw a line graph to show the statistics in **E**.
b What does your graph tell you about motorway traffic?
c Explain the advantages and disadvantages of motorways.

3 **a** Why was the M25 built?
b Why do you think the M25 has attracted more traffic than expected?
c The M25 cost over £1,000,000,000 to build. Briefly state whether you think the M25 should have been built. Give reasons for your answer.

4 Study **D**. There are three possible routes for a proposed motorway under discussion at a public enquiry. Write a report for the enquiry, listing the advantages and disadvantages of each route. End your report by stating your preferred route.

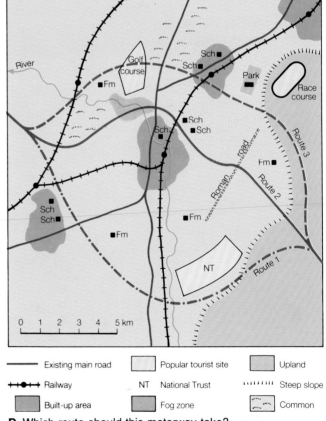

D Which route should this motorway take?

Key:
- Existing main road
- Railway
- Built-up area
- Popular tourist site
- NT National Trust
- Fog zone
- Upland
- Steep slope
- Common

	1970	1975	1980	1982	1983	1984
Motorways	9.5	20.5	27.5	29.0	31.0	35.0
All roads	209.5	244.7	247.5	259.4	264.4	274.6

E Traffic on motorways (thousand million vehicle km)
Number of vehicle km = number of vehicles using road × distance they travel

119

59 : Disaster at Chernobyl

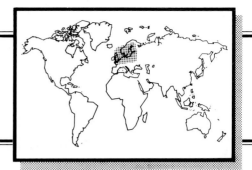

THE GREATEST FEAR of people living near nuclear power stations is that radioactivity will be released into the environment during an accident. Nuclear scientists have tried to calm these fears by stressing the safety features built into the power stations. However, they have accepted that small leaks of radioactive water or gases have occurred from time to time.

In 1979, a near-disaster occurred at Three Mile Island nuclear plant in Pennsylvania, USA. The whole plant was flooded with radioactivity and permanently closed. As a result, not a single new nuclear plant has been ordered in the USA since 1979, and those already under construction have been halted.

Nuclear Power In The Soviet Union

The Soviet Union has been a leading supporter of nuclear power for the last 30 years. By 1986, there were 71 nuclear power stations in the USSR, second only to the USA. Plans for expansion would increase the share of electricity generated in these stations from 10% to 20% by 1990 (**B**).

On 26 April, 1986 at 1.23 am, explosions occurred in the fourth reactor unit at Chernobyl near the city of Kiev. Two people were killed in the explosions. Radioactivity was released into the atmosphere when the reactor and the surrounding protective wall blew apart. Firemen who arrived on the scene could not use water or chemicals to put out the fires in the reactor. Eventually, helicopters had to be brought in to smother the fires with sand. Once the fires were extinguished, the plant was entombed in 300,000 cubic metres of concrete.

A After Chernobyl: evacuees in a new village

	1960	1980	1985
Natural gas	7.9	24.1	33.3
Oil	30.5	36.0	32.7
Coal	53.9	28.2	25.4
Hydro-electric power	1.0	6.0	3.2
Nuclear	—	1.1	2.9
Peat, shale, wood etc.	6.7	4.6	2.5

B Consumption of fuel and energy in the USSR (%)

	1980	1985	1990
Total	1294	1545	1860
Nuclear power	72.9	170	390

C Electricity generation in USSR (thousand million Kwh)

The After-Effects

- By the end of 1986, 31 people had died from the effects of radioactivity, and another 237 were in hospital with radiation sickness.
- Evacuation of the local area began on 27 April, starting with women and children. Altogether, 116,000 people had to be resettled.
- To house these evacuees, 12,000 new houses with allotments, roads and social amenities were built and 8,000 flats were taken over. New jobs also had to be provided and compensation paid for the damage caused.
- A 30 km wide zone was declared unsafe. 60,000 buildings had to be decontaminated. Tens of kilometres of dykes were built to prevent radioactive water seeping into rivers. Total cost was over £2 billion.
- In Kiev, a city of 2.5 million people, buildings were still being washed three times a day, and streets cleaned to remove radioactive dust, a year after the disaster. Checks with geiger counters were made on vehicles and crops entering the city.
- The sale of local milk and dairy products was banned. Top soil and dead leaves from trees were removed and buried as radioactive waste.
- The effects were also felt over much of western Europe as the radioactive cloud drifted with the wind (**E**). Places with high rainfall suffered most as the rain washed dust from the air onto the land. Even the reindeer pastures in Lapland (northern Scandinavia)

D Checking crops near Kiev with geiger counters

were affected. The animals were contaminated and became unfit to eat.

- In Britain, farmers in upland areas (**F**) were worst hit: more than 4 million sheep were affected at first. Prices for lamb fell as some sheep with high radioactive levels had to be slaughtered. By the end of 1986, there were still 180,000 sheep under restriction in the Lake District and North Wales. It was confirmed in 1987 that some radioactivity was still in the soil, and the new crop of lambs could not be sold.

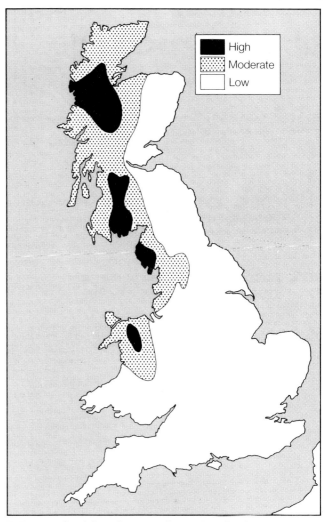

High
Moderate
Low

F Radioactive fallout from the Chernobyl cloud

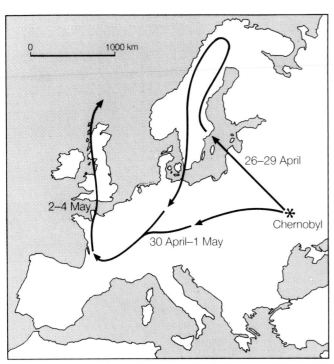

E The spread of the radioactive cloud after the Chernobyl accident on 26 April 1986

1 **a** Study **B**. Which sources of energy are becoming more important in the USSR, and which sources are becoming less important?
   b Draw a line graph to show the figures given in **C**. Use one line for total electricity generation and one line for nuclear generation.
   c What does your graph tell you about the changing importance of nuclear power in the USSR?
2 Copy the path of the Chernobyl radioactive cloud shown in **E** onto an outline map of Europe. Use an atlas to name the countries which were most affected by the cloud.
3 **a** Which parts of Britain received the most radioactive fallout from Chernobyl?
   b Explain why these areas received most fallout.
   c Which group of people in Britain were most affected?
   d How would the after-effects have been different if fallout had been heavy over the whole of Britain?
4 Re-read unit 53. The USSR and Britain intend to expand their nuclear power programmes. Do you agree with this policy? Explain the reasons for your answer.

121

60 : Taming the Nile (I)

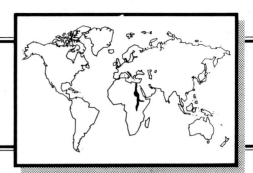

FOR THOUSANDS OF YEARS, the River Nile has been Egypt's lifeblood. Even today, nearly all of Egypt's population live along the banks of the Nile. Until the Aswan High Dam was completed in 1964, the annual river flood brought water for irrigation and deposited fertile silt on the nearby fields, enabling intensive food production in an otherwise arid wasteland without the use of expensive chemical fertiliser.

The flat fields on the flood plain were surrounded by low earth banks. When the river level was high during the annual flood, the water spread over the flood plain. It was held in the fields by earthen banks and used to irrigate the crops. This method was called **basin irrigation (B)**. When the river level was low, devices such as the shaduf, water wheel or archimedean screw were used to lift water over the banks (**E**).

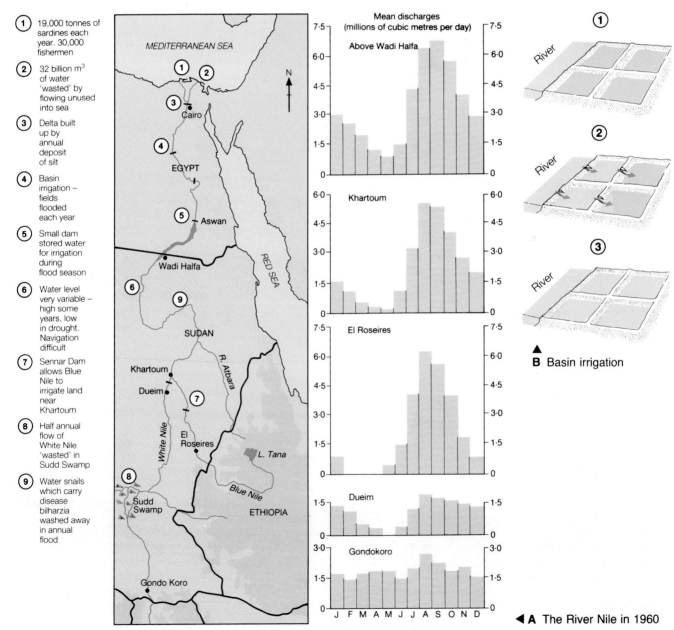

1. 19,000 tonnes of sardines each year. 30,000 fishermen

2. 32 billion m³ of water 'wasted' by flowing unused into sea

3. Delta built up by annual deposit of silt

4. Basin irrigation – fields flooded each year

5. Small dam stored water for irrigation during flood season

6. Water level very variable – high some years, low in drought. Navigation difficult

7. Sennar Dam allows Blue Nile to irrigate land near Khartoum

8. Half annual flow of White Nile 'wasted' in Sudd Swamp

9. Water snails which carry disease bilharzia washed away in annual flood

B Basin irrigation

◀ **A** The River Nile in 1960

Aswan	J	F	M	A	M	J	J	A	S	O	N	D
Temp (°C)	15	17.2	21.1	25.6	29.4	32.8	32.8	32.2	31.1	27.8	22.2	16.7
Rainfall					Practically nil							

C The Climate of Aswan

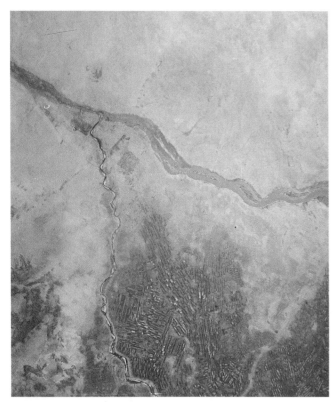

D The Nile valley from space

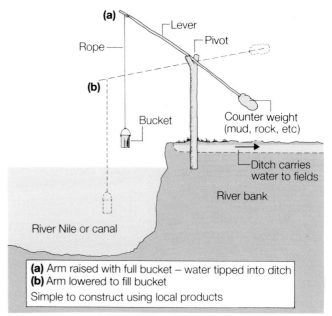

(a) Arm raised with full bucket – water tipped into ditch
(b) Arm lowered to fill bucket
Simple to construct using local products

E (i) The shaduf

1 **a** Draw a temperature graph for Aswan in Egypt.
b What type of climate does Aswan have?
2 **a** Study an atlas map of population density in Africa. Where do most of Egypt's population live?
b What is the population density (people per square kilometre) along the Nile valley?
c Why do so many people live along the banks of the Nile?
3 **a** Explain how a shaduf, water wheel and archimedean screw operate.
b Copy **B**, and label each diagram.
c Why was most of the Nile discharge said to be 'wasted'?
4 Study **A**.
a Describe the regime (varying discharge) of the White Nile at Gondokoro.
b By the time the Nile has reached Duiem, its discharge has changed dramatically. How, and why?
c At what time of year is discharge highest in the Blue Nile?
d How are the waters of the Blue Nile used by Sudan?
e At what time of year was basin irrigation possible?

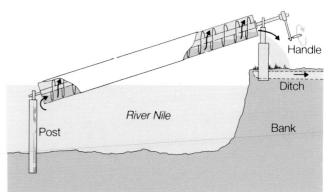

E (ii) The archimedean screw

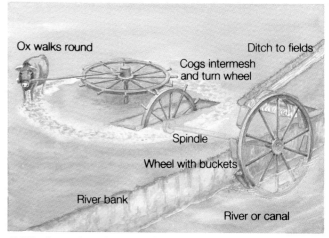

E (iii) Operation of a sakia (water wheel)

123

61 : Taming the Nile (II)

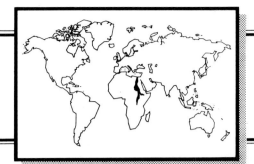

AS EGYPT'S POPULATION increased, the demand for water and food also increased. Larger and larger schemes were built during this century to control the Nile floods and utilise the precious silt of the narrow flood plain. Modern technology and foreign aid enabled the construction of the largest of these schemes, the Aswan High Dam, in 1964.

A huge reservoir 500 km long built up behind the dam, the second largest artificial lake in the world. It was called Lake Nasser after a famous Egyptian President. This reservoir stored the flood water for **perennial** (continuous) irrigation, rather than seasonal irrigation which only occurred when the river flooded.

Three-quarters of the stored water went to Egypt and one quarter to Sudan. A hydro-electric power station at the dam was built to meet growing demand for electricity in industry and rural areas. Money and technical help to build the dam were provided by the Soviet Union.

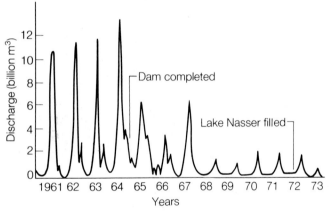

F The Nile discharge at the delta

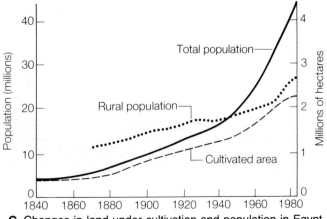

G Changes in land under cultivation and population in Egypt 1840–1981

① Sardine fisheries disappeared – less food for fish in Nile discharge

② Supply of silt cut off – coastal erosion up to 30 m per year

③ Spread inland of salt water – kills crops

④ Perennial (all year) irrigation possible. Two or more crops per year. No silt deposited, so increased use of fertiliser.

⑤ 400,000 Ha for farming reclaimed from desert. Food output increases

⑥ Spread of disease Bilharzia by snail which breeds in irrigation canals

⑦ Flow of river controlled. No disastrous floods or droughts

⑧ New dam supplies 47% of Egypt's electricity, enabling expansion of industry, spread of power to villages

⑨ Fish catch from reservoir 25,000 tonnes per year. 100,000 local people displaced and 20 historic temples flooded by reservoir

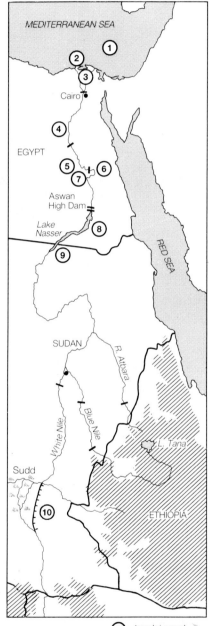

Water levels at record low due to drought and low flood surges

⑩ Jonglei canal begun to increase flow in White Nile and drain Sudd. Construction halted by civil war

H The Nile in 1987

124

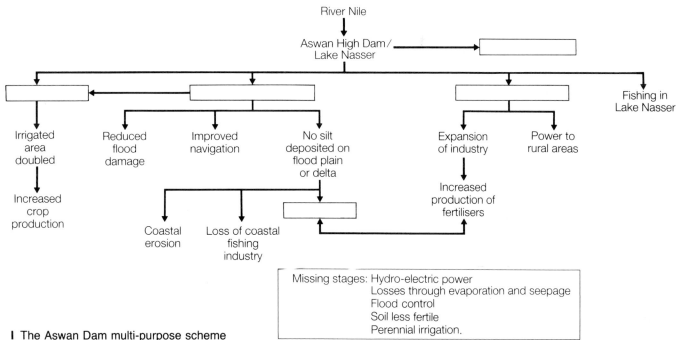

River Nile

↓

Aswan High Dam / Lake Nasser ————————→ [ ]

Irrigated area doubled ← [ ]

[ ] → Reduced flood damage

[ ] → Improved navigation

[ ] → No silt deposited on flood plain or delta

[ ] → Expansion of industry

[ ] → Power to rural areas

Fishing in Lake Nasser

Irrigated area doubled
↓
Increased crop production

Improved navigation / No silt → Coastal erosion

→ Loss of coastal fishing industry

No silt deposited on flood plain or delta ↓ [ ]

Expansion of industry ↓ Increased production of fertilisers → [ ]

Missing stages: Hydro-electric power
Losses through evaporation and seepage
Flood control
Soil less fertile
Perennial irrigation.

I The Aswan Dam multi-purpose scheme

1 Study the graphs and tables on these pages.
   a What was the population of Egypt in 1980?
   b How many years had it taken for the population to double to this figure?
   c What fraction of the population were still rural in 1980?
   d What effect did the Aswan Dam have on Nile discharge?
   e What effect did the Aswan Dam have on the silt load of the Nile?
   f What effect did the Aswan Dam have on crop yields (NB the dam was not completed until 1964).
   g What do you think was the MAIN reason the High Dam was built?
2 **a** In which country is the proposed Jonglei Canal?
   b Suggest why this canal is being built.
   c Why has construction stopped on this canal?
3 **a** Copy the flow diagram (**I**). Draw blue boxes around any advantages of the Aswan scheme, and red boxes around any disadvantages. Put these colours on a key underneath.

J The Aswan High Dam

b Add the five missing stages onto the flow diagram. Use the labels given below the diagram. Draw coloured boxes where appropriate.
c Make your own list of advantages and disadvantages for the scheme. Then write a report summarising your conclusions about the value of the Aswan scheme.

	J	F	M	A	M	J	J	A	S	O	N	D
Before	64	50	45	42	43	85	674	2702	2422	925	124	77
After	44	47	45	50	51	49	48	45	41	43	48	47

K Silt concentrations (parts per million) in the Nile, before and after construction of the Aswan Dam

Crop	1952	1962	1972	1982/83	Production unit
Wheat	12.80	1804	21.47	24.91	Ardeb
Maize	17.15	29.36	30.47	30.52	Ardeb
Rice	3.46	6.10	54.1	5.88	Ton
Peanuts	25.03	30.94	28.54	26.98	Ardeb

L Crop yields per hectare in Egypt

Glossary

Afforestation: the planting of trees.
Agribusiness: large scale modern agriculture and its associated activities.
Anticyclone: area of high atmospheric pressure.
Aquifer: permeable rock capable of holding water.
Arable: ploughed or fit for ploughing.
Artesian well: well sunk into permeable rock from which water is obtained at the surface with little, if any, pumping.

Bedding plane: surface where two layers of rock meet.
Bush fallowing: method of agriculture found in tropical Africa in which land is left unused for a period of time to restore fertility.

Condensation: process by which water vapour changes to liquid water when cooled.
Conservation: protection and preservation of the environment.
Conurbation: large continuous built-up area formed by growth of nearby towns.
Convection: process by which air or liquid rises when heated.

Deforestation: large-scale destruction of forest.
Deposition: laying down of sediment on sea bed, river valley etc.
Depression: area of low atmospheric pressure.
Desertification: spread of deserts through human activity.
Discharge: a measure of stream flow.
Drainage: removal of surplus water from land.

Ecosystem: system found in nature which links energy, soil, plant and animal life.
Environment: objects or region surrounding a person or place.
Epicentre: location of maximum earthquake damage.
Erosion: wearing away of rocks etc. as a result of movement by running water, glacial ice and wind.
Evaporation: process by which water changes to water vapour when heated.

Fault: large crack or fracture in Earth's crust.
Focus: site from which an earthquake originates.
Fossil fuel: fuel composed of remains of plant or animal matter eg oil, natural gas, coal.
Front: boundary between two air masses with different temperature and humidity.

Groyne: timber framework or low wall built to slow drifting of beach material.

Impermeable: rock or soil which does not allow water to pass easily through.
Irrigation: taking water to dry or arid land.

Joint: small crack found in some rocks eg granite, limestone.

Lava: liquid rock from volcano.
Levee: raised embankment alongside river or lava flow. May be natural or man-made.
Longshore drift: movement of beach material along shoreline as a result of wave action.

Mass movement: movement of soil or loose weathered material down a slope under the influence of gravity.
Meander: large bend in river.
Monsoon: seasonal wind found especially in south east Asia.

Nomad: person who wanders from place to place in search of food and water.
Nuée ardente: glowing cloud of hot gases emitted from some volcanoes.

Permafrost: layer of soil and rock which is permanently frozen.
Permeable: rock or soil which allows water to pass easily through.
Plate: section of Earth's crust which moves independently.
Polder: area of drained land found in Netherlands.
Pollution: destruction of the purity of the environment.
Population density: number of people divided by the area of land they occupy.
Precipitation: all of the methods by which water from the atmosphere reaches the surface eg rain, snow, sleet, drizzle.

Reclamation: recovery of unused land eg waste tips, mud flats.
Relief: shape of land surface, particularly height above sea level.
Reservoir: lake which builds up behind a dam.

Shanty town: area of sub-standard housing with no electricity, poor sanitation etc.
Shifting cultivation: moving to a newly cleared area of land when crop yield falls due to soil exhaustion.
Spit: long, narrow ridge of sand and shingle which grows out from the shoreline.

Subduction zone: region where one crustal plate is pushed beneath another crustal plate.
Subsistence farming: producing food for home consumption rather than for sale.

Terrace: step-shaped feature on hillside. Can be a natural feature caused by river erosion, or a man-made feature used for agriculture.
Transform fault: fracture where crust moves laterally (sideways) in opposite directions on either side of the fracture.

Transhumance: seasonal migration of livestock farmers and their animals between two regions with a different climate eg between valleys and uplands.
Transpiration: process by which plants give out water vapour.
Tsunami: giant wave produced by shaking of ocean floor during a volcanic eruption or earthquake.

Water table: upper limit of groundwater.
Weathering: breakdown of rock by elements of weather eg frost, rain, heat.

Index